BAKER'S POCKET BOOK
OF RELIGIOUS QUOTES

HUGH D. JOHNSON
1938 THORNHILL DRIVE
SOUTH BEND, IND. 46614

BAKER'S POCKET BOOK OF RELIGIOUS QUOTES

Albert M. Wells, Jr.
Editor and Compiler

BAKER BOOK HOUSE
Grand Rapids, Michigan

Whenever possible, the quotations in this volume have been credited as they appear. If copyrighted material has inadvertently been used without permission, the publisher requests that this information be forwarded so that proper acknowledgement can be made in future printings. Acknowledgements for several of the verse selections in this volume follow:

224 is taken from *Masterpieces of Religious Verse*, edited by James Dalton Morrison. Reprinted by permission of Harper & Row, Publishers.

417 is taken from "Stopping by Woods on a Snowy Evening," by Robert Frost in *Complete Poems of Robert Frost*. Copyright renewed © 1964, 1967 by Lesley Frost Ballantine.

927 is reprinted by permission of *The Pentecostal Evangel*.

989 is reprinted from the *Pentecostal Evangel*, by permission. Copyright © 1974 by the General Council of the Assemblies of God.

994 is reprinted by permission of *The Congregationalist*.

998 is reprinted by permission of the *Herald of Holiness*.

1069 is taken from *Halfway up the Sky*, by Jane Merchant, and is used by permission.

Copyright 1976 by
Baker Book House Company
ISBN: 0-8010-9575-1
Printed in the United States of America.

PREFACE

As editor of *Guide to Social Science and Religion in Periodical Literature* for ten years, it has been my privilege to read about one hundred thousand articles in both popular and scholarly periodicals. Very early in this assignment I realized that there was swiftly passing before my eyes an abundance of profound and pithy paragraphs, pregnant with wit and wisdom and much spiritual truth.

Out of this awareness grew a personal quote file for my own edification. And from this file comes *Baker's Pocket Book of Religious Quotes*.

While a small number of the entries in this volume come from non-Christian sources, none of the quotes are incompatible with the Christian faith. A few are unrelated to religion, but they do provide certain succinct insights that may be helpful.

At the end of the book and under the heading, "The Lighter Side," I have included certain puns and points of good humor. While these particular entries are for your sheer enjoyment, it is evident that ethical points can often be persuasively made in the context of humor. Perhaps in some instances this section will serve as "sugar to make the medicine go down."

My purpose in compiling this book is to provide brief quotations that bring into sharp focus Christian truths for spiritual edification. While the substance of truth comes from the Word which is paramount, the stimulus for accepting truth often comes from the words which comprise a profound thought.

At the close of this volume is a source list to help the reader determine from what source a quotation is taken. The numbers in this source list correspond to the number of the quotation in the text.

Admittedly, the entries chosen for inclusion in this book have a strong evangelical flavor since they reflect the prejudices, preferences, and presuppositions of the editor. However, one must remember, that in the process of selecting quotations, it is necessary to do so with a desire for sighting the author's point. The author of a short quotation has no way of defining terms or qualifying conclusions. So quotations are seldom universally absolute in their meaning, and not infrequently overstate the case to make a point.

It is a great joy for me to share these thought-provoking quotations which have brought so much help and understanding into my own life. I hope that you, too, will find them a great source of insight and inspiration.

Albert M. Wells, Jr.

ABORTION

1. You can scrape the baby out of the womb, but you cannot scrape the baby out of the mind.
Frank J. Ayd, Jr.

2. The difference between destroying "life" in a plant or animal and destroying life in a human fetus is that in human abortion life is destroyed that is destined to be, or determined to develop, into an eternal soul, irreversibly stamped with the image of God.

3. Abortions are performed by the thousands simply because people want the freedom of promiscuous sex but not the responsibility of children.
R. Eugene Sterner

4. Abortion is no more purely a medical problem just because the physician wields the curette than chemical warfare is purely a problem for pilots because they press the lever releasing the chemical.
E. Fuller Torrey

ACCOUNTABILITY

5. God drags us out, as it were, from everything we have sought to hide behind and turns into bright daylight the night in which we have tried to become personless and eliminate our responsibility.
Helmut Thielicke

ADDICTION

6. Addiction is an increasing desire for an act which gives less and less satisfaction.
Aldous Huxley

ALCOHOL

7. While millions have regretted tasting alcohol, no person will ever be sorry he rejected it.
Gordon Chilvers

8. Don't try to drown your sorrow in alcohol because sorrow is an expert swimmer.

Ann Landers

9. A drunk is a person who could stop drinking if he would. An alcoholic is a person who would stop drinking if he could.

Tom Shipp

10. No man ever drank lard into his tub, or flour into his sack, nor meal into his barrel, nor happiness into his home, nor God into his heart.

Benjamin Franklin

11. You cannot prove total abstinence from the Bible, but you can prove the wisdom of total abstinence both from the Scriptures and also from human experience.

L. Nelson Bell

12. The name of every saloon is "bar,"
     The fittest name by far;
     A bar to heaven, a door to hell;
     Whoever named it, named it well.
     A bar to manliness, a bar to wealth,
     A door to sorrow and broken health;
     A bar to honor, pride and fame;
     A door to sorrow, grief and shame.
     A bar to hopes, a bar to prayer;
     A door to darkness and despair;
     A bar to useful, manly life,
     A door to brawling, senseless strife.
     A bar to heaven, a door to hell;
     Whoever named it, named it well.

A convict, 25,
Joliet Prison
Joliet, Illinois

13. In ten years forty-six thousand Americans died in Vietnam. During that same time two hundred fifty thousand persons were killed in the United States by drunk drivers.

14. If alcoholism is a disease, then it is the only disease that is bottled and sold. And it is the only disease that is contracted by the will of man. It is the only disease that requires a license to propogate it. It is the only disease that requires commercial outlets to spread it.

If alcoholism is a disease, then it is the only disease that produces revenue for the government. And it is the only disease that provokes crime. It is the only disease that is habit forming. It is the only disease that kills multiplied thousands on the highways. It is the only disease that is spread by advertising, and it is the only disease without a germ or virus as its cause. Could it be that it's not a disease after all?

AMBITION

15. Unless a man undertakes more than he possibly can do, he will never do all he can do.

Henry Drummond

16. If you want to set the world on fire, try burning a little midnight oil.

17. The poor man is not he who is without a cent, but he who is without a dream.

Harry Kemp

AMERICA

(See: United States.)

ANGER

18. Anyone who angers you, conquers you.

Sister Kenney

19. Hot heads and cold hearts never solved anything.

Billy Graham

ANTI-CHRIST

20. The lines are drawn and multitudes are on the march. Satan has a dynamic movement in full swing. It hates God but imitates the church. The real issue today is not social, political, or economic. The real issue is Christ or anti-Christ. The choice is between God who became man or man who will play God.

APATHY

21. You can go to a football game, cheer yourself hoarse, and the world calls you a fan. But allow yourself to get a little excited about evil, immorality, and apostasy, and you are no longer a fan but a fanatic. Not wanting to suffer even the small stigma attached to the fanatic image, we more often than not steer clear of Christian action and limit our concern to a little harmless chit-chat on the church steps. In the meantime the nation continues to crumble and the world goes to Hell.

22. E. Stanley Jones described slightly religious people by saying that they had been innoculated with a mild

form of Christianity and thus rendered immune from the real thing.

23. Most people in the pews are like people sitting in an airline terminal. They hear announcements of arrivals and departures, watch all the hurry and bustle, and imagine they are really in on the action, yet they never purchase a ticket or board the plane.
Samuel M. Shoemaker

24. The Christian faith has not been tried and found wanting. It has been found difficult and left untried.
G. K. Chesterton

25. An insistent puritan is often disturbing, but one who is lukewarm is disgusting.

26. It often appears that we evangelical Christians today do not hotly pursue or passionately embrace the fundamentals of our faith. Neither, however, do we choose to plunge into the cold waters of crass worldliness. Instead, we end up somewhere in the middle—a batch of tasteless, odorless, and colorless dough—half-warm, half-cold, half-baked, half-hidden, and only half-eaten half of the time by half of the people who, themselves, become half-hearted.

27. The greatest waste in the world is the difference between what we are and what we could be.
Ben Herbster

28. Most of us are sufficiently wise and cautious to stay far enough from crucifixions till they are over, and then generously and graciously vote the victims a place among the honored dead.
Billy Graham

29. The average American lets his boss think for him at work, his television for him at home, and his pastor thinks his theology for him on Sunday. The most he taxes his brain is trying to figure out the next play his favorite football team will run.
David Gillespie

30. That this world is a playground instead of a battleground has now been accepted in practice by the vast majority of fundamentalist Christians.
A. W. Tozer

31. Jesus went about doing good. It is surprising how many of His followers are satisfied with just going about.
Aya Kagawa

32. What confronts us is a world so shaken by revolutionary men, minds and movements that Christians who opt for noninvolvement are in effect the monastics of the day. Their disengagement will not enhance their gospel witness. It will isolate it. It will make it remote and oddly hollow, like shouting into an empty barrel.
Paul S. Rees

33. A Roman soldier asked Julius Caesar for permission to commit suicide, so as to put an end to his miserable and meaningless existence. He was a dispirited person, without any vitality. Caesar paused to size him up carefully and then asked: "Man, were you ever really alive?"

34. The hottest places in hell are reserved for those who, in a period of moral crisis, maintain their neutrality.

Dante

35. The real corrupters of society may be, not the corrupted, but those who held back the righteous leaven, the salt that has lost its savor.
J. H. Thom

36. Get to church sometime. Don't panic. Sitting in a pew is no commitment. You couldn't be safer. Most Christians spend more time on their butts than on their knees anyway. If they ever had to stand up for what they believe, their legs would collapse.
Suzanne Wieger

37. He trespasses against his duty who sleeps upon his watch, as well as he that goes over to the enemy.
Edmund Burke

38. If I profess with the loudest voice and clearest exposition every portion of the truth of God except precisely that little point which the world and the devil are at that moment attacking, I am not confessing Christ, however boldly I may be professing Him. Where the battle rages, there the loyalty of the soldier is proved, and to be steady on all other battlefields besides is mere flight and disgrace if he flinches at that point.
Martin Luther

ASPIRATION

39. Aim at heaven and you get earth thrown in. Aim at earth and you get neither.
C. S. Lewis

40. We ain't what we ought to be, and we ain't what we want to be, and we ain't what we're going to be. But thank God—we ain't what we was.

41. A man's reach should exceed his grasp, else what's a heaven for?

Robert Browning

ASSURANCE

42. The cardinal warned Luther not to oppose the pope: "The pope's little finger is stronger than all of Germany. Do you expect your princes to take up arms to defend you—you, a wretched worm like you? I tell you, no, and where will you be then?" Luther replied: "I'll be right where I am now—in the hands of God."

ATHEISM

43. Man is powerfully drawn to thought systems like astrology, natural evolution, and atheism because impersonal power makes no moral demands.

ATONEMENT

44. My entire theology can be condensed into four words: "Jesus died for me."

Charles Spurgeon

B

BACKSLIDING

45. The Christian life is like an airplane. When you stop, you drop.

46. People become lost not by design . . . but because they become involved in their own patch of grass and nibble themselves out of sight.
G. Curtis Jones

47. When you are growing in grace you are hard on and critical of yourself. On the other hand, when you are backsliding you are hard on and critical of others.

48. Vice is a monster of such frightful mien,
     As, to be hated, needs but to be seen.
     But seen too oft, familiar with her face,
     We first endure, then pity, then embrace.
Alexander Pope

49. If you find yourself loving any pleasure better than your prayers, any book better than the Bible, any house better than the house of God, any table better than the Lord's table, any person better than Christ, any indulgence better than the hope of heaven—take alarm!
Thomas Guthrie

BALANCE

50. I'm very careful with the cup;
    I daren't play the clown.
    I know that if I live it up,
    I have to live it down.
Gertrude Leigh

51. No man has a right to lead such a life of contemplation as to forget in his own ease the service due to his neighbor; nor has any man a right to be so immersed in active life as to neglect the contemplation of God.
Saint Augustine

THE BIBLE

52. As tears come from the heart and appeal to the heart, so the Bible comes from God, and he that is from God listens to its voice.

Michael Faraday

53. I want to know one thing—the way to heaven.... God himself has condescended to teach the way. He hath written it down in a Book. Oh, give me that Book. Here is knowledge enough for me. Let me be a man of one Book.

John Wesley

54. The Christians who have turned the world upside down have been men and women with a vision in their hearts, and the Bible in their hands.

T. B. Maston

55. It is impossible to mentally or socially enslave a Bible-reading people.

Horace Greeley

56. To the prayerful explorer of its pages, the Bible always reveals its credentials.

J. Sidlow Baxter

57. The bulwark of the church is the man who is well grounded in Scripture.

Jerome

58. Do not try to make the Bible relevant. Its relevance is axiomatic.

Dietrich Bonhoeffer

59. Man can live by bread alone—if it's the Bread of Life.

A. J. Amick

60. No man is uneducated who knows the Bible and no one is wise who is ignorant of its teachings.

Samuel Chadwick

61. There will be no skeptics in hell. Neither atheists, infidels, or agnostics. Eternity will make everyone a Bible-believer.

62. The less the Bible is read, the more it's translated.

C. S. Lewis

63. And weary seekers of the best,
   We come back laden from our quest,
   To find that all the sages said
   Is in the book our mothers read.

John Greenleaf Whittier

64. I am sorry for men who do not read the Bible every day. I wonder why they deprive themselves of the strength and the pleasure.

Woodrow Wilson

65. Most people are bothered by those passages of Scripture which they cannot understand. But, as for me, I have always noticed that the passages in Scripture which trouble me most are those which I do understand.

Mark Twain

66. Pilgrims came to America to establish a social order in which the governing principle would be that a man with the Bible in his hand doesn't need a king to tell him what to do.

G. Aiken Taylor

67. If you do not believe you will not understand.

Saint Augustine

68. Despite the cynic's angry word,
    The skeptic's narrow look,
    The running ages have not matched
    This holy, mighty Book.

Lon Woodrum

69. I have heard a few Greek scholars say that when they first read Plato, they found it a mirror for their souls. That may be. But they never found in Plato salvation from their sins, nor a sinless Redeemer, nor the absolute assurance of eternal life and of resurrection after death. Only the Bible offers you that.

Wilbur Smith

70. The fate of the Bible is the fate of Christianity.

Emil Brunner

71. Nobel Prize winner, Robert A. Millikan, the first to isolate the electron and measure its charge, said: "I suspect that the future progress of the human race will be determined by the circulation of the Bible."

72. Read it through; pray it in; live it out; pass it on.

George Gritter

73. If God calls us to preach His Word we should not stoop to be worldly kings.

Clifford Chew, Jr.

74. Unless we form the habit of going to the Bible in bright moments as well as in trouble, we cannot fully respond to its consolations because we lack equilibrium between light and darkness.

Helen Keller

75. A knowledge of the Bible without a college education is more valuable than a college education without the Bible.

William Lyon Phelps

76. To do God's work we must have God's power. To have God's power we must know God's will. To know God's will we must study God's Word.

John R. Mott

77. The answers we find in the Bible are not quick or easy answers, but they are in fact the only real answers.

78. Whom God intends to destroy He gives leave to play with the Scripture.

Martin Luther

BROTHERHOOD

79. I sought my soul, but my soul I could not see; I sought my God, but my God eluded me; I sought my brother, and I found all three.

80. Nothing my brethren think or do will ever be as important to me as the foot of the cross that makes them my brethren.

W. Carl Ketcherside

BRUTALITY

81. A beast does not know that he is a beast, and the nearer a man gets to being a beast, the less he knows it.

George MacDonald

BUSINESS AND INDUSTRY

82. What most employers are looking for today is alert young people between the ages of twenty-two and thirty-five with forty years of experience.

83. The aim of all legitimate business is service, for profit, at a risk.

Benjamin C. Leeming

84. Incorporation is often "the act of uniting several persons into one faction called a corporation, in order that they may no longer be [held] responsible for their actions."

Ambrose Bierce

C

CAPITAL PUNISHMENT

85. There is no juster law than that the contrivers of death should perish by their own contrivances.

Ovid

CENSORIOUSNESS

86. Some critics are like chimney sweepers: they put out the fire below, and frighten the swallows from their nests above; they scrape a long time in the chimney, cover themselves with soot, and bring nothing away but a bag of cinders, and they sing out from the top of the house as if they had built it.

Henry Wadsworth Longfellow

87. Most of us would get along very well if we used the advice we give to others.

88. You have to be little to belittle.

89. Some people who never touch intoxicating liquor are, nevertheless, dead drunk with pride, and the wild use of their lips reveals the totality of their self-intoxication.

Haydon L. Gilmore

90. Prayer is the most cleansing therapy of the heart and the soul. It converts the "halitosis of hateful speech" into the clean, kind, pure breath of the Spirit.

Carl W. Franke

91. Criticism is often a form of self-boasting.

92. Linus of "Peanuts" fame: "I love mankind; it's just people I can't stand."

93. When we're concentrating on evangelism we don't have time to pick at other Christians and their faults.

Paul Little

94. When you are growing in grace you are hard on and critical of yourself. On the other hand, when you are backsliding you are hard on and critical of others.

95. I am the master of the unspoken word. But once that word is spoken I become its slave.

Arthur A. Link

96. An egoist isn't all bad. At least he doesn't go around gossiping about other people.

97. If you add enough dirt, you can make a mountain out of almost any molehill.

98. The faults of others are like headlights on a car. They always seem to glare more than your own.

99. He who wants only friends without faults will be without friends.

100. The person who has a sharp tongue soon cuts his own throat.

101. The trouble with most Christians today is that they would rather be on the judgment seat than on the witness stand.

CHANGE

102. Most of the change we think we see in life is due to truth being in and out of favor.

Robert Frost

103. Everybody thinks of changing humanity and nobody thinks of changing himself.

Leo Tolstoy

104. Patterns of the past and novelties of the present are equally unreliable guidelines. Both must be scrutinized by Scripture and utilized on the basis of their adjudged merit.

105. Some people are like crawfish. They back into their future while looking at their past.

106. Christians who know the relevancy of both the past and the future will not appreciate or appropriate fads that come and go. The disciple embraces a double fixation: the Resurrection of the past and the Rapture of the future. On this couplet he predicates the present.

107. That we must "change with the times" is the modern church's final self-deception.

108. There are some churches where the board is so much in favor of maintaining the status quo that if they had been present at the creation they would have voted for chaos because it was there first.

109. When we start out to change the language of the Gospel, we usually end up changing the Gospel.

110. The world is changing. And it should be changing. The problem arises over whether the changes taking place are for the better or the worse. When judged by the standards of the Bible, most contemporary changes are clearly for the worse.

111. Change doth unknit the tranquil strength of men.
Matthew Arnold

112. We are not bored at things simply because they are old, the same, or frequently experienced. We are bored because we do not care for them.
Lon Woodrum

113. A whole generation of religious thinkers is busy cutting itself loose from history and tradition and casting away both the forms and faith they consider too old to be valid.

CHARACTER

114. Life is a grindstone, and whether it grinds a man down or polishes him up depends on the stuff he's made of.
Josh Billings

115. I do the very best I know how—the very best I can; and I mean to keep doing so until the end. If the end brings me out all right, what is said against me won't amount to anything. If the end brings me out wrong, ten angels swearing I was right would make no difference.
Abraham Lincoln

116. When I think of those who have influenced my life the most, I think not of the great but of the good.
John Knox

117. God give us men! A time like this demands
   Strong minds, great hearts, true faith and ready hands;
   Men whom the lust of office does not kill;
   Men whom the spoils of office cannot buy;
   Men who possess opinions and a will;
   Men who have honor; men who will not lie.
Josiah Gilbert Holland

118. There is no power on earth that can neutralize the influence of a high, pure, simple and useful life.
Booker T. Washington

119. The trouble with most of us is that we would rather be ruined with praise than saved by criticism.

120. Always do right. This will gratify some people and astonish the rest.

Mark Twain

121. Not how did he die?
But how did he live?
Not what did he gain?
But what did he give?
These are the units to measure the worth
Of a man as a man regardless of birth.
Not what was his station?
But had he a heart?
And how did he play his God-given part?
Was he always ready with words of good cheer,
To bring back a smile and to banish a tear?

122. Our deeds still travel with us from afar,
And what we have been makes us what we are.

123. What you laugh at reveals what you are.

124. If I must choose between peace and righteousness, I choose righteousness.

Theodore Roosevelt

125. Beauty is spirit deep.

Gordon Wetmore

126. The quality of our faith determines the character of our conduct.

Wayne Geisert

127. Character is not a single quality but a three-dimensional achievement built on the foundation of decision, direction, and dedication.

(See also: Honesty; Integrity; Interpersonal Relations.)

CHARITY

128. When we worry about somebody getting something for nothing, let him who has never himself got something for nothing be the one to throw the first stone.

Kenneth L. Wilson

129. Not what we give, but what we share,
For the gift without the giver is bare,
Who gives himself with his alms feeds three,
Himself, his hungering neighbor and Me.

130. W. Carl Ketcherside tells of being conducted through a beautiful church where the carpet alone cost thousands of dollars. As he passed the bulletin board a

poster caught his eye. It pictured an emaciated human form with peering eyes. Looking more closely he noticed a typewritten note posted to the picture: "Help raise $50 for starving children."

CHILDREN

131. Curiosity is a clever device nature invented to teach children how little their parents really know.

CHOICES

132. We all take masters, even when we think ourselves most on our own. Choose yours with discrimination, for . . . each master will take all you have to give in energy and allegiance.

Lester DeKoster

(See also: Priority.)

CHRISTIAN ACTION

133. Our grand business is not to see what lies dimly at a distance, but to do what lies clearly at hand.

Thomas Carlyle

134. We do not see the vital point,
That 'tis the eighth most deadly sin,
To wail, "The world is out of joint,"
And not attempt to put it in.

135. General William Booth of the Salvation Army once said: "If anyone wants to join the Salvation Army, let him don a uniform and get to work. If he doesn't want to do that, let him join a church and sit in a pew."

136. The road to holiness necessarily passes through the world of action.

Dag Hammarskjold

137. From compromise and things half-done,
Keep me, with stern and stubborn pride;
And when at last the fight is won,
God, keep me still unsatisfied.

Louis Untermeyer

138. The roads we take are more important than the goals we announce. Decisions determine destiny.

Frederick B. Speakman

139. Do all the good you can, in all the ways you can, to all the people you can, as long as ever you can.

John Wesley

140. The "Acts" of the Apostles is the title of one New

Testament book. Their "resolutions" have not yet reached us.

141. Faith is not trying to believe something regardless of the evidence. Faith is daring to do something regardless of the consequences.

142. According to our Lord, faith will indeed move mountains, but planting a few mustard seeds must surely be a prior consideration.

143. Prayer never excuses sloth. And neither does prayer excuse a lack of initiative. Prayer that does not lead one to action is little more than blasphemy. This point is effectively made in a prayer by Sir Thomas More: "Those things, good Lord, that we pray for, give us also the grace to labor for."

144. A shouting mob can make a great deal of noise and create much fear. But a silent, disciplined marching body of men, stepping out in dynamic and creative action can accomplish impossible goals.

145. In the Chinese alphabet, the character for *crisis* is a combination of the symbols for *danger* and *opportunity*. A crisis demands action in the face of danger.

146. I am willing to go anywhere so long as it is forward.

David Livingston

147. If not now, when? If not you, who? If not God's way, how?

148. The hottest places in hell are reserved for those who, in a period of moral crisis, maintain their neutrality.

Dante

149. Billy Sunday, after being criticized by a non-involved female faultfinder, said: "You're right, madam. I don't like my method either. But I like my way of doing it wrong better than your way of not doing it at all."

150. Good is never done except at the expense of those who do it; truth is never enforced except at the sacrifice of its propounders. At least they expose their inherent imperfections, if they incur no other penalty; for nothing would be done at all if a man waited till he could do it so well that no one would find fault with it.

John Henry Newman

151. The times upon which we have fallen are indeed evil. So far as we are responsible—and we are in some

measure responsible—we can do some constructive things to improve the times. And what we can do, we have a moral imperative to do.

152. You can go to a football game, cheer yourself hoarse, and the world calls you a fan. But allow yourself to get a little excited about evil, immorality, and apostasy, and you are no longer a fan but a fanatic. Not wanting to suffer even the small stigma attached to the fanatic image, we more often than not steer clear of Christian action and limit our concern to a little harmless chit-chat on the church steps. In the meantime the nation continues to crumble and the world goes to Hell.

153. A dog barks when his master is attacked. I would be a coward if I saw that God's truth is attacked and yet would remain silent.

John Calvin

(See also: Involvement; Service.)

CHRISTIAN EDUCATION

154. A presupposition of Christianity is that a Christian is in possession of the truth. That being so, it necessarily follows that Christian parents and teachers are committed not only to the instruction of children, but to indoctrination as well—since the ultimate battle in life is truth against non-truth.

CHRISTIAN FREEDOM

155. The wisdom of the Decalogue is irrefutable and man is most free when he walks under God's law.

156. There is no absolute freedom. You either live under the bonds of sin and guilt, or you operate within the confines of God's laws freely.

157. Until you are free to die, you are not free to live.

158. When we accept Christ we are free to do what we must.

159. We must be anchored in self-discipline if we are to venture successfully in freedom.

Harold E. Kohn

160. A born-again believer living in a slave state is freer by far than an unsaved American living in the land of the free.

161. You are free to choose, but you are not free to choose the consequences of your choices—and you are not free to cease being free.

CHRISTIAN HOME

162. If Christianity is not working well in the home, what right have we to suggest it will work elsewhere?

163. Christian family living is ... the gospel most intimately made real.

Nels F. Ferre

164. The oldest and grandest calling in the world is building a Christian home.

165. The family circle is the supreme conductor of Christianity.

Henry Drummond

(See also: The Family; Marriage; Parenthood.)

CHRISTIANITY

166. The Christian faith is a religion. But unlike other religions, you do not possess Christianity. Instead, Christianity, and therefore Christ, possesses you. Consequently, you become, not so much a religious person, but a "personal religion." This personal religion which you become is not to be confused with private religion. Rather it is personal because your relationship to God is person to person, and it is religion because that relationship is absolute in commitment.

167. While all genuine Christianity embraces religious experience, it does not follow that all religious experience embraces genuine Christianity.

168. Show the world the fruits of Christianity and it will applaud. Show it Christianity and the world will oppose it vigorously.

Watchman Nee

169. The strangest truth of the Gospel is that redemption comes through suffering.

Milo L. Chapman

170. One thing Christianity cannot be is moderately important.

C. S. Lewis

171. Christianity can be condensed into four words: admit, submit, commit, transmit.

Samuel Wilberforce

172. If the community imagination is so fertile as to believe that the Christian faith is a figment of that collective imagination, why then do major religions not spring up every century under the stimulus of some

character with popular ideas and an aura? Why not with Gandhi? Or why didn't the legends about Robin Hood get him off the ground?

J. Norby King

173. The Christian religion teaches men two truths: that there is a God whom men can know, and that there is a corruption in their nature which renders them unworthy of Him.

174. The Gospel brings abundance of life, and also death at the stake; freedom, and also imprisonment; peace, and also the sword.

175. I believe in Christianity as I believe in the sun—not only because I see it, but because by it I see everything else.

C. S. Lewis

176. The Christian faith has not been tried and found wanting. It has been found difficult and left untried.

G. K. Chesterton

177. The church has been so busy making Christianity acceptable that we've failed to make it authentic. Authentic Christianity seeks power, not to enhance one's position, but to endure hardship for Jesus' sake.

178. The Christian faith offers peace in war, comfort in sorrow, strength in weakness and light in darkness.

Walter A. Maier

179. A religious man is one whose life is directed toward something he considers more significant than everything else. The Christian is one whose religion is devotion to Jesus Christ.

180. The Christian faith is a faith—not a philosophy, not a psychology, not a human welfare program, not a system of government, nor an institution. It is a faith.

181. No one is excluded from the Gospel but many are excluded by the Gospel.

Karl Barth

(See also: Christian Freedom; Christian Life; The Church; Discipleship.)

CHRISTIAN LIFE

182. The Christian's joy is not feelings of perpetual pleasure but a comforted sorrow. The Christian is symbolized, not so much by beating a drum in a public

parade, but by one who travels toward Calvary with a deep concern in his heart.

183. The Christian life is like an airplane. When you stop, you drop.

184. Good for the body is the work of the body, and good for the soul is the work of the soul, and good for either is the work of the other.

Henry David Thoreau

185. Everything that happens to me can help me along in my Christian life.

E. Stanley Jones

186. Spiritual growth soars when we have prayed up, made up, and paid up.

187. Purity of heart is to will one thing.

Soren Kierkegaard

188. It is far less important to die the martyr's death than to live the martyr's life.

Robert E. Speer

189. We need to lose our spiritual fat in order to strengthen our spiritual faith so as to insure a spiritual future.

190. There are three areas that must be cultivated if any faith is to be a living faith: the inner life of devotion, the intellectual life of rational thought, and the outer life of human service.

D. Elton Trueblood

191. If we Christians seek to avoid all criticism . . . we will have to resign ourselves to the role of "taxidermined" Christians.

Eva Cummings

192. I live for those who love me,
    For those who know me true,
    For the heaven that smiles above me,
    And awaits my spirit too;
    For the cause that lacks assistance,
    For the wrong that needs resistance,
    For the future in the distance,
    And the good that I can do.

George L. Banks

193. The bitterest cup with Christ is better than the sweetest cup without Him.

Ian MacPherson

194. Jesus invested His life in you. Have you shown any interest?

195. Religion is grace and ethics is gratitude.
R. Newton Flew

196. Christian living is not fighting for a position but from a position.
Paul O. Kroon

197. We may always be sure, whatever we are doing, that we cannot be pleasing God if we are not happy ourselves.
John Ruskin

198. Whatever we desire . . . will be Dead Sea fruit in our mouths unless we remember that God comes first.
Joy Davidman

199. The Bible is not a handbook of nonresistance. The love of Christ is voluntary steel, not forced spongework.
David Redding

200. A real Christian is an odd number. He feels supreme love for one whom he has never seen. He talks familiarly everyday to someone he cannot see, expects to go to heaven on the virtue of another, empties himself in order that he might be full, admits he is wrong so he can be declared right, goes down in order to get up. He is strongest when he is weakest, richest when he is poorest, happiest when he feels worst. He dies so he can live, forsakes in order to have, gives away so he can keep, sees the invisible, hears the inaudible, and knows that which passeth knowledge.
A. W. Tozer

201. If you find yourself loving any pleasure better than your prayers, and any book better than the Bible, any house better than the house of God, any table better than the Lord's table, any person better than Christ, any indulgence better than the hope of heaven—TAKE ALARM.
Thomas Guthrie

202. No man has a right to lead such a life of contemplation as to forget in his own ease the service due his neighbor; nor has any man a right to be so immersed in active life as to neglect the contemplation of God.
Saint Augustine

203. The genuine Christian life is unspoiled by prosperity and unbroken by adversity.

204. A Christian is someone who shares the sufferings of God in the world.

Dietrich Bonhoeffer

205. There are no traffic jams on the straight and narrow way.

206. The mature Christian is in God's will. He doesn't have to find it. He only has to live it.

207. God grant me the serenity to accept the things I cannot change, the courage to change the things I can, and the wisdom to know the difference.

208. The process of Christ [Christ-like development] makes all would-be substitutes taste like sawdust.

Mary Morrison

209. The greatest Christian alive is still the palest imitation of Christ.

Phyllis K. Miller

210. To be much like Christ, be much with Christ.

Charles Spurgeon

211. Christians are funny when they are phony, but they are regal when they are real.

Leonard Verduin

212. Spiritual maturity is the point at which we cease to rationalize our sins and begin to symbolize our faith.

213. What you are is God's gift to you. What you become is your gift to God.

214. While God treats us [Christians] as if we had never sinned, we must never treat God as if we had never sinned.

Oscar F. Reed

215. The decisive test of one's belonging to Christ is not reception of baptism, nor partaking of the Lord's Supper, but solely and exclusively a union with Christ through faith which shows itself active in love.

Emil Brunner

CHRISTIAN SERVICE

(See: Service.)

CHRISTIAN WITNESS

216. If you can't turn your faith into the vernacular, then either you don't understand it or you don't believe it.

C. S. Lewis

217. As the person who doesn't know how to count never has any mathematical problems, so the Christian who doesn't witness never has any persecutions. And both will fail in their respective testings.

218. If your faith isn't contagious, it must be contaminated.

Chester Johnson

219. Once we become children of God, we must learn to act like it.

Robert W. Battles

220. A genuine Christian ought to be as distinguishable amongst his fellows as is a civilized man among savages.

Hugh McIntosh

221. Someone has said: "You ought to be able to tell a Christian by the way he climbs a tree." That might seem a bit far-fetched. After all, is there a Christian way to do math? Bake bread? Yes, there is. It is not without reason to assume that a person's most intimate, precious, and powerful commitment, whatever it might be, will lend a certain color and tone to anything he does.

John L. May

222. Observing that nonwitnessing Christians have become the norm while witnessing Christians are too often the exception, Tom Nees has likened the modern church to an insurance company without salesmen.

223. Christian faith is like breath. If you hold it, you die.

224. We are the only Bible
The careless world will read;
We are the sinner's gospel,
We are the scoffer's creed.
We are the Lord's last message,
Given in deed and word—
What if the line is crooked?
What if the type is blurred?

Annie Johnson Flint

225. It is the secret wish of every person to be well thought of. So we often shrink from carrying our Christian witness to the point of creating hostility, which usually means we shrink from witnessing.

226. Pictures tell a story
That many words cannot,

And lives that glow with love for Christ
Put sinners on the spot.

227. Example is not the main thing in influencing others—it is the only thing.

Albert Schweitzer

228. Do you seriously suspect that the "telling of Jesus" has lost its punch? If it has, then that is God's problem and not yours or mine. But if the telling of Jesus has not lost its punch, then this means that we are not "telling Jesus"—and this is our problem.

229. A single drop of water will not quench the thirst of everyone in the desert, but it does prove that there is such a thing as water. And your individual Christian witness will not affect the salvation of every man you meet, but it does prove that God's gift of grace is not only real, but in real possession of the believer's heart.

230. Letting your Christian light shine in an un-Christian world is never dull or unexciting.

231. The early Christians did not say: "Look what the world has come to," but "Look what has come to the world."

E. Stanley Jones

232. Too much light upon a poor reflector is its sure destruction.

Jack Conn

233. The embattled Christian should always remember that any serious witness for Christ will always be considered by the Devil as deserving of attack.

234. When men see in us, by comparison, the distortion of their sinful character, we have been a true mirror of Christ. But when in us they see no censure of their own sinful mindset, we have reflected to them an image of truth as distorted as their own carnal nature.

235. There is no such thing as a Christian who does not witness.

236. If Christianity is to compete in the marketplace where social options strive for men's allegiance, Christians must witness there.

237. Witnessing is not a spare-time occupation or a once-a-week activity. It must be a quality of life. You don't go witnessing, you are a witness.

Dan Greene

238. Every non-Christian is an emergency waiting for a Christian to act.

Barbara Webb

239. If you were on trial for being a Christian, would there be enough evidence to convict you?

240. We Christians must say to a devil-dominated world "I am a Christian" in such a way that worldlings hear it. They won't like it, but they must hear it. And if we bear the hostile consequences in a Christ-like manner, some will be saved.

241. We can hardly be messengers of good news unless Jesus Christ is the best news we've ever had. That kind of experience is hard to suppress.

Philip Wahlberg

242. The trouble with most Christians today is that they would rather be on the judgment seat than on the witness stand.

CHRISTMAS

243. That there was no room in the inn was symbolic of what was to happen to Jesus. The only place where there was room for Him was on the Cross.

William Barclay

244. If we were determined to conceal and subvert the Gospel, it would be hard to invent a better device than the Santa myth.

John Mahoney

245. At Bethlehem God became what He was not before, but did not cease being what He always was.

Paul Lowenberg

246. God risks guilt by association and imparts innocence by association with His own act in the gift of Jesus, whom people call the Christ.

247. The cuddly, cooing infant in the manger may evoke warm feelings and sentimental thoughts at Christmas time. But the Man of Galilee has a message and a mission which we dare not lose in an ocean of wrapping paper. . . .

Erwin A. Britton

248. Christmas turns all wise souls from the surface which is time to the center which is eternity.

E. Merrill Root

249. Howard Nemerov scathingly describes Christmas as the "annual savior of the economy."

250. He who has not Christmas in his heart will never find it under a tree.

Roy L. Smith

251. Our trouble is we want the peace without the Prince.

Addison H. Leitch

THE CHURCH

252. The Church is content not style, mastery not dilettantism, the body of Christ not people in an elevator. To turn from the Church because it lacks style is like jumping from an oceanliner because you disliked its onboard music.

Joseph Bayly

253. The true Church is the restraint of evil in the land. When that restraint is lifted by compromise with the world, evil takes over.

Theodore H. Epp

254. We tend to meet any new situation by reorganizing, and a wonderful method it can be for creating an illusion of progress, while producing confusion, inefficiency, and demoralization.

Petronius Arbiter

255. The tragedy of the Christian churches today is that they can continue to exist as "institutions" when the spiritual life has gone out of them. Over the centuries, all the major churches have developed a number of secondary functions and resources which enable them to continue to exist, and in some cases to appear to prosper, without in the least fulfilling the task that Christ assigned to them.

H. O. J. Brown

256. The church without power is a factory for hypocrites.

Samuel M. Shoemaker

257. Ninety percent of our churches get started on the wrong foot. We go through the usual round of organization: rent a building, call a pastor, build the first unit, increase the budget, proliferate organizations, add a second wing, and hire more staff. The result is a Christian ghetto run by paid professionals.

Robert L. Roxburgh

258. What the soul is to the body, that are Christians to the world.

Mathetes

259. The first duty of the church is not to evangelize but to get ready to evangelize.

Vance Havner

260. If the Holy Spirit were withdrawn from the church, 95 percent of our activities would continue and we would brag about it.

Samuel M. Shoemaker

261. It is not the compromise of the cautious but the blood of the martyr which is the seed of the Church.

262. Many failures of the contemporary church may be traced to one particular failure—the failure to seize and maintain cultural initiative instead of aping the world.

263. The Church is not a savior, but the fellowship of those who have found a Savior.

264. Wherever we see the Word of God purely preached and heard, there a church of God exists, even if it swarms with many faults.

John Calvin

265. The church, for its part, can never become indifferent to symbols. It depends for its very identity on their explicit and conscious use.

Richard Luecke

266. Before the church can be a heavenly company it must first be an earthly army.

267. The standards of a Boy Scout troop are higher than those of many churches. If you miss four times at your service club—you're out. If you miss your dues at the country club—you're out. If you continually fail to show up for work—you're fired. Maybe it's time for the church to get tough. If we don't demand something, we'll get anything—which is frequently nothing.

268. When the church undertakes to proclaim the Christian gospel in a secular idiom, it usually ends up proclaiming the secular gospel in a Christian idiom.

269. If the church insists on looking like the world, dressing like the world, acting like the world, and living like the world, it will be difficult to convince the worldling that we have anything to offer which he doesn't already have in greater abundance.

270. The reason the church has not invaded the world is because the world has invaded the church.

271. Every effort employed by the church must be judged by one criterion—does it really bring men to Jesus Christ?

272. The church doesn't need your gift half as much as you need to give.

273. An organization and a name do not make a church. One hundred persons organized do not constitute a church any more than eleven dead men make a football team.

A. W. Tozer

274. The early disciples were fishers of men, while modern disciples are often little more than aquarium keepers.

275. The ecumenicals are moving ahead with impressive speed because believing little, they correspondingly differ about little.

Malcolm Muggeridge

276. The danger of the church is not that it will be unsuccessful—but that it will succeed in that which is unimportant.

277. The church spends too much of its time trying to make non-Christians act like Christians.

L. Nelson Bell

278. Too often the church continues to announce faith while it has mostly discontinued demonstrating it.

279. The words of Cyprian, Bishop of Carthage, written in the third century are as timely today as when he wrote them. He said: "If I could ascend some high mountain and look out over this wide land, you know very well what I would see. Robbers on the high roads, pirates on the sea; . . . selfishness and cruelty, misery and despair under all roofs. It is a bad world, an incredibly bad world, but in the midst of it I have found a quiet and holy people who have learned a great secret. They are despised and persecuted, but they care not. They are the masters of their souls. They have overcome the world. These people are the Christians and I am one of them."

280. I think that I shall never see
A church that's all it ought to be;
A church whose members never stray
Beyond the straight and narrow way;

> A church that has no empty pews,
> Whose pastor never has the blues;
> A church whose deacons always "deak,"
> And none is proud, and all are meek;
> Where gossips never peddle lies
> Or make complaints or criticize;
> Where all are always sweet and kind,
> And all to others' faults are blind;
> Such churches perfect there may be,
> But none of them are known to me;
> But still, I'll work and pray and plan
> To make my own the best I can.

281. The late distinguished Dean of St. Paul's Cathedral in London, William R. Inge, once noted that complaints were being made concerning empty churches. The dean remarked: "I can think of some churches which would be even emptier if the Gospel were preached in them."

282. The church—almost anybody's version of it—may look fearsomely organized from the outside, but once you're in it, you have to be deaf, dumb, and blind to avoid the conclusion that it is the most disorganized venture ever launched. Its public image may be that of a mighty lion on the prowl; but what it really is, in this day and age at least, is a bunch of not too well co-ordinated pussycats falling all over each other.

Robert F. Capon

283. The modern church is not making much of an impact on the world, but the world is making a devastating impact on the church.

284. Never before have we had so many degrees in the church and yet so little temperature.

Vance Havner

285. When the line separating citizenship of this world with citizenship of the heavenly Kingdom is blurred or removed, the church is soon in trouble.

Joseph Bayly

286. Denominations, as we know them, are not evil; they simply are not important. There is no harm in their continued existence and they may do some good that would not be done otherwise. But they are no longer central in the Christian stream; they occupy the side channels. It is as inept to condemn the side channel as it is to spend one's life limited to it.

D. Elton Trueblood

287. The church has been so busy making Christianity acceptable that we've failed to make it authentic. Authentic Christianity seeks power, not to enhance position, but to endure hardship for Jesus' sake.

288. New Testament churches were not perfect but they had a standard and it was not imperfection. They tried to live up to their standard and they dealt with anybody who tried to lower it.

Vance Havner

289. Someone should inform the contemporary church that the time has come to cease defining Christianity and begin demonstrating it.

290. The church will come into a golden era any time she decides to honor the Holy Spirit.

Richard Ellsworth Day

291. Don't look for the perfect church. You'll never find it. And even if you did, you couldn't qualify for membership.

292. There is the nagging possibility that the institutionalized church is more difficult to dismantle than real Christianity is to restore. Both appear increasingly necessary and equally unlikely.

293. The post-Easter church has a pre-Easter mission in a world not yet raised from the dead. It was as hard for the old Israel to accept a suffering Messiah as it is for the new Israel to accept its role as suffering servant.

Wilfred Winget

294. Why is it that God does not allow an organization to remain pure for more than one generation?

William Booth

295. If the church maintains her separation from the world, she will always be despised. If she ever becomes popular, it will be a sign of compromise.

Reuel G. Lemmons

296. The trouble with the nation is not that the nation is corrupt. (Nations are always corrupt.) The trouble with the nation is that the church is corrupt.

G. Aiken Taylor

297. It does not take a perfect church to introduce a man to the perfect Christ.

Richard Woodsome

298. In the contemporary church the obsession to grasp

the glamor of innovative techniques serves only to mask our own emptiness.

299. When church people are born again, "programs" aren't necessary. If they are not new born, programs won't help.

300. You don't see the church on Sunday morning any more than you see the army when it's on dress parade.
Bill Popejoy

301. The fellowship of the church is based not upon the common cars, cares, or conflicts of its members, but upon their common faith. Christian community is found, not in sharing the most recent sports thrill or trading the latest housekeeping or lawn-care tips, but in sharing our Christian concerns and rejoicing together in spiritual victories.

302. As individual Christians are lured into the activities of a non-Christian system, the hierarchy or boards of the church will have to come on strong with programs and gimmicks to retain the interest of its members and to feed its economy. Increasingly one will hear the words of success and salesmanship rather than obedience and discipleship. Some "faith giving" plans are already presented in such a way as to rival the religious tricks of Rev. Ike. It is not difficult to imagine that evangelism will soon be made an end in itself rather than one of the means that God has provided to call his own.

Elwood Bass

303. If the church would dare to preach and practice the things which Jesus Christ commanded, she would soon regain her lost power.
Washington Gladden

CITIZENSHIP

304. Whatever makes men good Christians, makes them good citizens.
Daniel Webster

305. Bad officials are elected by good people who don't vote.
Edmund Burke

CIVILIZATION

306. Maybe civilization is dying; but it still exists, and

meanwhile we have our choice: we can either rain more blows on it, or try to redeem it.

Saul Bellow

307. I am not sure whether ethical absolutes exist. But I am sure that we have to act as if they existed or civilization perishes.

Arthur Koestler

308. The major advances in civilization are processes which all but wreck the societies in which they occur.

Alfred North Whitehead

309. When hell drops out of religion, order drops out of society.

310. I used to say that civilization was going to the dogs. But I've quit saying that out of respect for the dogs.

Vance Havner

311. Civilization is always in danger when those who have never learned to obey are given the right to command.

Fulton J. Sheen

COMMITMENT

312. The world has yet to see what God can do with a man who is fully and wholly consecrated to Him.

Henry Varley

313. A lady once said to Fritz Kreisler: "I'd give my life to play a violin as you do!" His amazing answer was: "Madam, I did."

314. The prayer of commitment must be a way of life—not just a despairing cry at the end of failure.

315. "What has to be will be" is no more Christian commitment than a faucet drip is rain. Much of what we call "dedication to God's will" is often only rebellion that has run out of gas.

316. Any commander who fails to obtain his objective, and who is not dead or severely wounded, has not done his full duty.

George S. Patton

317. Christian commitment is no shipwreck; it's the navy yard of the future. The ark of salvation has always been invincible and you can be sure that the situation will not change this side of the New Jerusalem no matter how hard the worldly winds may blow.

318. In forty years I have not spent fifteen waking minutes without thinking of Jesus.

Charles Spurgeon

(See also: Duty.)

COMMUNICATION

319. A lack of communication is in fact a form of communication. It speaks of a deep need in someone's life for substantial spiritual help.

320. I know you believe you understand what you think I said, but I am not sure you realize that what you heard is not what I meant.

321. If language is not correct, then what is said is not meant. If what is said is not meant, then what ought to be done remains undone.

Confucius

322. You might as well talk nuclear physics to a cigar store wooden Indian as to talk spiritual things to a person who hasn't been born again.

Vance Havner

323. No sentence of any depth or significance can be shouted.

D. Elton Trueblood

COMMUNISM

324. In case you think the United States has not succumbed to the double whammy of Communism and socialism, be advised that according to Kenneth Galbraith our government expenditures in 1974 accounted for a greater proportion of economic activity in the U.S. than government expenditures in the socialist countries of India, Sweden, and Norway. And our government expenditures measure the same proportion as in Communist Poland.

325. Communism flourishes only where patriotism does not.

J. Kesner Kahn

326. Society cannot leap into Communism from capitalism without going through a socialist stage of development. Socialism is the first stage to Communism.

Nikita S. Khrushchev

327. We [Communists] must hate—hatred is the basis

of Communism. Children must be taught to hate their parents if they [the parents] are not Communists.

Nikolai Lenin

328. No, we [Communists] shall not institute violence; all we shall do is to make the maintenance of existing civil order impossible, and then its defenders will have either to use violence or surrender. Bourgeios gentlemen, you shoot first.

Friedrich Engels

329. Communism, which preaches equal distribution of wealth, always results in complete distribution of poverty.

330. People who want to change democracy for socialism are blind. Life in Russia is a nightmare which has to end sometime.

Svetlana Stalin Alliluyeva

331. Rational dissent is as American as apple pie. Irrational [violent] dissent is as Communistic as the hammer and sickle.

William O'Donnell

332. Demoralize the youth of a nation and the revolution is already won.

Nikolai Lenin

333. Socialism will work only in two places: in heaven where it's not needed, and in hell where they already have it. Capitalism is the unequal distribution of wealth. Socialism is the equal distribution of poverty. Communism is nothing but socialism with a gun at your back.

Winston Churchill

334. When the capitalist world starts to trade with us—on that day they will begin to finance their own destruction.

Nikolai Lenin

335. A Communist is a fellow who envies your successes and wants to tear you down to his level so he will not need to envy you.

336. A revolution is not a banquet; it is not like writing a poem or sketching a design or doing embroidery. A revolution cannot be conducted with elegance, tranquility or delicacy; it does not allow the least softness, kindness, courtesy, restraint or magnanimity. A revolu-

tion is an upheaval, an act of violence in which one class rises against and puts down another.

Mao Tse-tung

337. Communism is moral cancer and you cannot peacefully coexist with cancer. Either you get the cancer or the cancer gets you.

Vance Havner

COMPASSION

338. When you help someone else up the hill, you reach the top yourself.

339. We evangelicals will fight the liberals when they say there is no hell, but we ... don't take the risk of opening our homes to those going there in an effort to rescue them.

Francis A. Schaeffer

(See also: Love.)

COMPLACENCY

(See: Apathy.)

COMPROMISE

340. The failure to vigorously reject falsehood and evil is soon followed by the failure to accept truth and righteousness.

341. Each appeaser hopes if he feeds the crocodile enough, the crocodile will eat him last.

Winston Churchill

342. We insult God when we compromise faith to make it acceptable to this age.

Vance Havner

343. If I see definite signs of great danger on the evangelical horizon but compromise my convictions for a mess of popularity porridge, I have capitulated to the cunning of Satan and become his unwitting but unceasing accomplice.

344. The worldlings, for lack of Biblical orientation, are following the radicals. And the liberals, for lack of spiritual discernment, are following the worldlings. And the evangelicals, for lack of Christian commitment, are following the liberals. In other words, the evangelical is following the liberal who is following the worldling who is following the radical who is following the Devil into a deep and deadly ditch.

345. Sometimes with secret pride I sigh
To think how tolerant am I;
Then wonder which is really mine,
Tolerance, or a rubber spine.

Ogden Nash

346. The true Church is the restraint of evil in the land. When that restraint is lifted by compromise with the world, evil takes over.

Theodore H. Epp

347. When the Lord's sheep are gray, all the black sheep feel more comfortable.

Vance Havner

CONFORMITY

348. None but blockheads copy each other.

William Blake

349. Ours is the age of the image industries; we don't see people, we see patterns. More important than owning a late model car is being a late model cat. Even the freaks come in standards. That's how Jesus freaks can make the scene.

Edmund P. Clowney

350. He who would marry the spirit of the age soon becomes, not a widower, but a prisoner.

351. We often call for commitment to Christ and settle for conformity to a conventional code.

Leon Morris

CONSCIENCE

352. A conscience is that impediment which so often rudely interrupts while money is talking.

353. The human conscience is like the police; it may be eluded, stifled, drugged, or bribed. But not without cost.

Karl Menninger

354. Men always find it easier to substitute the ceremonial aspects of religion for the demands of a clear conscience before God.

James M. Boice

355. Two things hold me in awe; the starry heaven above me and the moral law within me.

Immanuel Kant

CONTENTMENT

356. Be content with what you have but not with what you are.

357. For you and me Canaan is a state of mind. We take our Promised Land not by making a long journey, but by learning to be content.

Keith Huttenlocker

358. "I find in whatsoever state I am therewith to be content." This would not mean so much were it not for the fact that it was uttered by a man who was unfairly treated, unjustly jailed, and finally was a victim to the executioner's axe.

359. For the Christian who has learned, with St. Paul, "in whatsoever state I am therewith to be content," there is nothing in the world that a bended knee at the throne of Grace will not take care of.

(See also: Happiness; Peace of Mind.)

CONVERSION

360. Give a man a dollar and you cheer his heart. Give him a dream and you challenge his heart. Give him Christ and you change his heart.

Neil Strait

361. A man can accept what Christ has done without knowing how it works; indeed he certainly won't know how it works until he's accepted it.

C. S. Lewis

362. No man can ever enter heaven until he is first convinced he deserves hell.

John W. Everett

363. He maketh me to search for meaning
  Where it is never found,
  He leadeth me through human deserts
  O'er dry and thirsty ground.
  Yea, though I strive to righteous be,
  His temptations are defeating me.
  Only when I come to the valley of the shadow,
  Do I begin to understand
  That he prepareth a trap for me
  With the cooperation of my enemies.
  He dulleth my head with flatteries;
  My cup of troubles runneth over.
  Surely, sin and sorrow will follow me the rest of my life.
  And I shall dowell in the halls of hell—forever, . . .
  Unless I submit to the rod of repentance to God,
  And find the right path away from His wrath,
  Where riches untold shall be mine manyfold,

In the forgiveness of sin with Christ coming in.
Praise God! I've been found! The Good Shepherd is mine,
I do not and I shall not want.

364. It is hard for the worldling to accept Christ because "following" Christ appears hard to him from his abnormal perspective. He is used to predicating decisions on illusion (devil's lies) instead of on reality (God's truth). Therefore, he accepts the illusion that following Christ is most difficult. So accepting Christ—which is quite simple—becomes a tough issue, since for him the illusion dies hard.

365. A former drug addict and recent convert, upon contemplating his new station in life, said: "When I accepted Jesus as my Savior, no one told me I was also accepting the Devil as my enemy."

366. It won't save your soul if your spouse is a Christian. You've got to be something more than an in-law to Christ.

Billy Sunday

367. You have to be born spiritually before you grow up spiritually.

368. Conversion is not an internal rearrangement of attitudes based upon some external suggestion. The changes that are seen in the lives of those who become Christians are due to the implantation and subsequent outworking of the Holy Spirit.

David Morley

369. The radical demands of Christ are made to free us from the confounding troubles of a divided heart.

370. Conversions by trick or promise, by force or fear, by ignorance or custom—such conversion is not possible. People are converted in mind and spirit or not at all. Water doesn't convert. The Holy Spirit converts that person who after free investigation of the claims of Christ says: "I'm sorry for my sins, and I'm going with God."

(See also: New Birth; Salvation.)

CONVICTION

371. Never, for sake of peace and quiet, deny your own experience or convictions.

Dag Hammerskjold

372. What a man believes, he will die for. What a man merely thinks, he will change his mind about.

373. The hottest places in hell are reserved for those who, in a period of moral crisis, maintain their neutrality.

Dante

374. Give me the benefit of your convictions if you have any, but keep your doubts to yourself, for I have enough of my own.

Johann Wolfgang Goethe

COUNTER CULTURE

375. The majority of peoples in modern times have followed a vision that can loosely be named after the Greek god Apollo—the god of light, moderation, reason, order, balance, and boundaries. A minority have followed Dionysus, the god of wine, excess, fantasy, and metamorphosis. Now the tables are turning. Dionysians are fast becoming a majority in strength, numbers, and influence.

376. The new generation is ungovernable by anyone, though old-style governments still don't realize what has hit them.

Alex Comfort

COURAGE

377. Fear isn't cowardice. Cowardice is failure to fight fear. The weakling feels fear and quits. The man of courage feels fear and fights.

Arnold Glasow

378. Life is mostly froth and bubbles;
Only two things stand like stone.
Kindness in another's troubles,
Courage in your own.

379. Courage is a special kind of knowledge: the knowledge of how to fear what ought to be feared and how not to fear what ought not to be feared.

David Ben-Gurion

380. Courage is the victory of faith over fear.

381. The hero is no braver than an ordinary man, but he is brave five minutes longer.

Ralph Waldo Emerson

382. Sometimes courage shrinks so small,
We wonder if it's there at all.
But then when there's a real demand,
It stretches like a rubber band.

383. There is a thin line between not being afraid and not being overconfident. One might call this tightrope courage—and it demands great and careful balance.

384. Men who fear God face life fearlessly. Men who do not fear God end up fearing everything.
Richard C. Halverson

385. Courage is fear that has said its prayers.

386. More important than the good life is the good death, and the only good death is the Christian death, which follows a Christian life.

COWARDICE

387. Cowards die many times before their deaths; the valiant taste of death but once.
William Shakespeare

388. Silence is not always golden; sometimes it's just plain yellow.

389. Mob courage is cowardice.
Gladys Hunt

CREATION

390. No life per se has been isolated. Because of the threshold's vanishing, those chemists who are preoccupied in synthesizing the particular atomically structured molecules identified as the prime constituents of humanly employed organisms, if chemically successful, will be as remote from creating life as are automobile manufacturers from creating drivers of their automobiles.
R. Buckminster Fuller

391. The theory of evolution has numerous "ifs"; but the Christian creation theory has no "ifs," which makes it, of course, much more than a theory.

392. There was a professional critic who even found fault with God and His creation. Talking one day beneath a giant oak tree and near a garden, he told a friend how the acorn should be on the end of the fragile pumpkin vine and the pumpkin on the sturdy oak tree. Just then an acorn fell from the tree under which he was standing and hit him on the head. His friend asked: "Now do you still wish the acorn had been a pumpkin?"

393. Creation is not more complex than we think it is. It is more complex than we can think!

CRIME

394. There is no juster law than that the contrivers of death should perish by their own contrivances.
Ovid

395. Crime will continue to rise until society in general and the courts in particular transfer their preoccupation from the rights of the villain to the rights of the victim.

396. We are focusing tender concern on the criminal while ignoring the cries of his victims.
J. Edgar Hoover

397. Crime costs us a great deal every year, but we certainly get a lot for our money.

398. The tendency to blame guns for crime is as ridiculous as blaming pencils for misspelled words.
Wallace F. Bennett

CRITICISM

(See: Censoriousness.)

THE CROSS

399. Those who preach the cross of our Lord Jesus are the terror of modern thinkers. In their hearts they dread the preaching of the old fashioned Gospel, and they hate what they dread.
Charles Spurgeon

400. The Cross is not a weight that bears you down; it is a supernatural symbol that gives you strength and speeds your way.

401. The Cross is the finger of God on the real sore of humanity—a sinful heart.

402. Christ's Cross is the sweetest burden that ever I bare; it is such a burden as wings are to a bird or sails to a ship.
Samuel Rutherford

(See also: Good Friday Theme.)

CYNICISM

403. I hate cynicism a great deal worse than I do the devil; unless, perhaps, the two were the same thing.
Robert Louis Stevenson

404. Sour godliness is the devil's religion.
John Wesley

D

DEATH

405. Dying men have said that they were sorry that they had lived as an atheist, skeptic, agnostic, or sinner; but no man has ever said on his deathbed: "I'm sorry that I'm a Christian."

406. Death is the great adventure, beside which moon landings and space trips pale into insignificance.

Joseph Bayly

407. You can doubt God out of your schools, you can write God out of your books, you can rule God out of your nation, and you can laugh God out of your life; but you cannot ignore God out of your death. For most this is too late learned, but no less lethal.

408. If we had to face death about once a month, what great Christians we would be.

409. I have seen the moment of my greatness flicker.
   I have seen the eternal Footman hold my coat and snicker,
   And in short, I was afraid.

T. S. Eliot

410. Only those who plan for death are really prepared for life.

411. No man is an island, entire of itself; every man is a piece of the Continent, a part of the maine. . . . Any man's death diminishes me, because I am involved in mankind; therefore, never send to know for whom the bell tolls; it tolls for thee.

John Donne

412. Time goes, you say? Ah, no! Alas, time stays, we go!

Henry A. Dobson

413. If through faith in Christ you can claim with Saint Paul victory over the awful specter of death, you stand invincible against both puns and persecution.

414. When you've made you body a residence for Jesus, there is no shock in dying.

415. I have provided in the course of my life for everything except death; and now, alas! I am to die entirely unprepared.

Caesar Borgia

416. Death takes no bribes.

Benjamin Franklin

417. The woods are lovely, dark and deep,
But I have promises to keep,
And miles to go before I sleep.

Robert Frost

DECEPTION

418. The louder he talked of his honor, the faster we counted our spoons.

Ralph Waldo Emerson

419. The confession of a small truth sometimes covers a huge deception.

420. The nearer a lie is to the truth, the more deceitful it is.

DEFEAT

(See: Backsliding; Failure.)

DEMOCRACY

(See: Politics and Government.)

THE DEVIL

421. When Charles G. Finney was asked how he could believe in a devil, he retorted: "Why don't you try opposing him sometime and you'll find out whether he exists or not."

422. The Devil's greatest asset is the doubt people have about his existence.

John Nicola

423. The Devil tries to shake truth by pretending to defend it.

Tertullian

424. If Satan can induce men to regard him as a joke, it is easy to make them follow blindly in his deadly wake.

L. Nelson Bell

425. I believe Satan to exist for two reasons: first, the Bible says so; and second, I've done business with him.
Dwight L. Moody

426. If Satan didn't exist he'd have to be invented to satisfy the demand for him.

DISCERNMENT

427. Earth's crammed with heaven
And every common bush afire with God;
But only he who sees takes off his shoes—
The rest sit round it and pluck blackberries.
Elizabeth Barrett Browning

428. Christians do not pass judgment on the personal standing of others with God, but they do pass judgment on the public effect of a particular witness or testimony.
G. Aiken Taylor

DISCIPLESHIP

429. If someone's sense of security depends on having all men speak well of him he can never be secure in following Christ.

Calvin Miller

430. Christianity is more than obstetrics. It is pediatrics, public health, internal medicine, diagnostic care, surgery, and geriatrics. In short, it is a life of discipleship. Years after Jesus had gone to be with the Father, His followers were still known as disciples. You never outgrow the need to listen, learn, follow, and lead.
Jamie Buckingham

431. Discipleship is not dynamic until it is willing to be despised by the world. Furthermore, discipleship is not dynamic until it *is* despised by the world. And the converse is equally true. Discipleship is not despised by the world until it is dynamic.

432. If to serve God meant unfailing prosperity and unruffled serenity, then people would serve God for none but selfish reasons. But discipleship is more than "decidedship"—Christian discipleship includes staying power.

DISCIPLINE

433. The greatest firmness is the greatest mercy.
Henry Wadsworth Longfellow

434. The Christian principles are, admittedly, stricter than the others; but then we think you will get help

towards obeying them which you will not get towards obeying the others.

C. S. Lewis

435. There can be the "taut" or the "loose" bonds of discipline. A little winking at the rules here, a growing laxity there; perhaps a mental reservation at one time and neglect of proper procedures at another—and lo, you have a "loose" ship. Flabby discipline girds no one very well for battle, neither militarily nor spiritually.

436. We are in bondage to the law in order that we may be free.

Cicero

437. The difference between "somebody should" and "I will" is self-discipline.

Pollyanna Sedziol

438. In a day of innovative idolatry, it should be remembered that the touchstone of the Christian faith is not freedom but discipline.

439. We must be anchored in self-discipline if we are to venture successfully in freedom.

Harold E. Kohn

DISHONESTY

440. A father, upon learning that his son had stolen several pencils from a department store, scolded him severely and said: "You ought to know better than to steal. I can pick up all the pencils you need at the office."

DISSENT

441. Rational dissent is as American as apple pie. Irrational [violent] dissent is as Communistic as the hammer and sickle.

William O'Donnell

442. The decline of laughter is one of the saddest results of over-acceptance of protest as a style of life.

D. Elton Trueblood

DIVINE GUIDANCE

443. The Holy Spirit expects us to take seriously the answers He has already provided, the light He has already shed; and He does not expect us to plead for things that have already been denied.

Paul Little

DIVINE HEALING

444. It is more important, more thrilling, more satisfying, and infinitely more valuable to know the Healer than to be healed.

445. Love, reconciliation, forgiveness, prayer—these are forces in the healing process. And if they do not always restore a person to health—they restore him to God which is infinitely more important.

DIVORCE

446. It may seem quite a distance from divorce American-style to euthanasia Nazi-style, but they both stem from an unprincipled ethic which elevates individual desires above the common good.

Gerald Reed

DOUBT

447. Give me the benefit of your convictions if you have any, but keep your doubts to yourself, for I have enough of my own.

Johann Wolfgang Goethe

DUTY

448. If we take to ourselves the wings of the morning and dwell in the uttermost parts of the sea, duty performed or duty violated is still with us, for our happiness or our misery.

Daniel Webster

449. The consideration that human happiness and moral duty are inseparably connected will always continue to prompt me to promote the former by inculcating the practice of the latter.

George Washington

450. Routine may not be the most glamorous element in our day, but no one gets very far without it.

451. Any commander who fails to obtain his objective, and who is not dead or severely wounded, has not done his full duty.

George S. Patton

(See also: Commitment.)

E

EASTER

452. Christians out-die pagans and the resurrection of Christ is the reason.

T. R. Glover

453. The post-Easter church has a pre-Easter mission in a world not yet raised from the dead. It was as hard for the old Israel to accept a suffering Messiah as it is for the new Israel to accept its role as suffering servant.

Wilfred Winget

454. Big news of Easter: Jesus Christ is risen!
Big question of Easter: Have you seen Him?

455. The one important thing was the reality of the living Christ in the disciples' midst. Apart from this experience, no argument for the Resurrection could be convincing; with it no argument is needed.

ECONOMICS

456. Prosperity is only an instrument to be used; not a deity to be worshiped.

Calvin Coolidge

457. A capitalist is one who has somehow managed to spend less than his income.

458. Poverty is a contagious disease, and the IRS is its major carrier.

Steven Symms

459. Pump priming there may need to be. But when the pump must be primed to the extent that more water goes in than comes out again, then it seems to the simple soul that we are not operating a well but trying to fill a bottomless pit.

W. T. Purkiser

460. The trouble with state [welfare] money is that experience shows it is often a bridge to nowhere.

461. Every time the government shifts a little to the left, the decimal point in taxes and the national debt shifts a little to the right.

462. Nothing that is morally wrong can ever be economically right.

Frank Linder

463. A poor person curses the capitalist until he becomes one. Likewise, a capitalist often ignores the poor until he becomes one.

ECUMENISM

464. The ecumenical movement brings back a vivid childhood memory of about twenty people reeling out of the pub door. They all had their arms around each other's shoulders, because if they didn't they would fall down.

Malcolm Muggeridge

(See also: Unity.)

EDUCATION

465. Having bent over backwards to separate church and state in lower schools and maintain academic freedom in higher education, modern man has filled the value-vacuum with secular religion. Its creed is: man is God; reason is truth; values are relative; and means are ends.

David L. McKenna

466. Culture of intellect, without religion in the heart, is only civilized barbarism and disguised animalism.

Robert Wilhelm Bunsen

467. An abominable unfamiliarity among young people with the nature of our culture-heritage shows that the schools are engaged in something other than the transmittal of the wisdom of the past.

Marjorie Holt

468. All education is religious.

Alfred North Whitehead

469. Plato said of certain teachers in his own day, [that they] condescend to the young, aping them in manner and dress lest one be thought authoritarian.

Charles Frankel

470. Education without religion, as useful as it is, seems rather to make man a more clever devil.

C. S. Lewis

471. The better part of every man's education is that which he gives himself.

James Russell Lowell

472. We spend ten thousand dollars for a school bus so children won't have to walk. Then we spend one hundred thousand dollars for a gym so they can get some exercise.

473. Commencement is the end of education—the beginning end. That's why it's called commencement.

474. Since we taught our young people that they came from animals, now they're acting like it.

Howard P. Courtney

475. Young people today are either being taught the wrong values or not being taught the right ones. So, given this circumstance, the degeneration of society will continue, if not by design, then by default.

476. One of man's worst temptations is "cleverness without character." The Duke of Wellington knew well the meaning of this premise when he said: "If you teach the three 'R's' and leave out the most important 'R'—Religion, you'll end up with a fourth 'R'—Rascaldom: a nation of clever devils."

477. A true education aims to implant a love of knowledge; an adherence to truth because it is truth; a reverence for man because he is a man; an enthusiasm for liberty; a spirit of candor, of breadth, of sympathy; and above all, a supreme regard for duty.

H. L. Wayland

478. Much of today's secular education is nothing more than a constant if not desperate attempt to rationalize man's natural, unregenerate, and increasingly destructive behavior.

EMOTION

479. Emotional mountain peaks are skirted about with deep chasms of doubt and despair.

480. The man who screams at a football game but is distressed when he hears of a sinner weeping at the cross

and murmurs about the dangers of emotionalism, hardly merits intelligent respect.

W. E. Sangster

ENCOURAGEMENT

481. If you wish to be disappointed, look to others. If you wish to be downhearted, look to yourself. If you wish to be encouraged . . . look upon Jesus Christ.

Erich Sauer

ENTHUSIASM

482. Enthusiasm is knowledge on fire.

Bill Wood

ENVIRONMENT

483. The ideal environment does not guarantee perfect performance. Remember, Adam was in paradise when he fell.

Vance Havner

ENVY

484. Every time you turn green with envy, you are ripe for trouble.

485. Aristotle defined envy as sorrow at other men's prosperity.

ETHICS

486. It may seem quite a distance from divorce American-style to euthanasia Nazi-style, but they both stem from an unprincipled ethic which elevates individual desires above the common good.

Gerald Reed

(See also: Interpersonal Relations.)

EVANGELISM

487. Our prayers for the evangelization of the world are only bitter irony so long as we only give our lip service and draw back from the sacrifice of ourselves.

M. Francois Goillard

488. According to statistics given at the 1966 Berlin Congress On Evangelism, the winning of one new member to the church in America requires the combined efforts of six pastors and one thousand church members for one year.

489. The first duty of the church is not to evangelize but to get ready to evangelize.

Vance Havner

490. Dost thou see a soul with the image of God in him? Love him, love him. Say to thyself, "This man and I must go to heaven together someday."
John Bunyan

491. We shall have all eternity in which to celebrate our victories, but we have only one short hour before the sunset in which to win them.
Robert Moffat

492.   Some wish to live within the sound
        Of church or chapel bell.
        I want to run a rescue shop
        Within a yard of hell.
Charles T. Studd

493. The Church is under orders. Evangelistic inactivity is disobedience.
John R. W. Stott

494. We need the kind of evangelism which tells a man that God is indispensable, Christ is available, and eternity is inevitable.

495. If we all become more Christlike, we shall not need any other bait.
Frank Crossley

496. An ancient proverb: "Because I have been athirst, I will dig a well that others may drink."

497. Pray for a good harvest, but keep on hoeing.

(See also: Personal Evangelism.)

EVOLUTION

498. The theory of evolution has numerous "ifs," but the Christian creation theory has no "ifs," which makes it, of course, much more than a theory.

EXPERIENCE

499. Experience is what you have left over after you make a mistake.

500. Good judgment comes from experience and experience comes from poor judgment.

501. Experience is recognizing a mistake the second time you've made it.

F

FAILURE

502. A great many people go through life in bondage to success. They are in mortal dread of failure. I do not have to succeed. I have only to be true to the highest I know—success or failure are in the hands of God.
E. Stanley Jones

503. Risk is what life is all about. Even failure is an opportunity to risk again, but with more experience.

504. Failure is not sweet, but it need not be bitter.

505. It is wrong if we become so obsessed with our failure that we forget the majesty of our Master.
James S. Stewart

506. The only really fatal element in defeat is the resolution not to try again.
J. H. Jowett

507. Failure is not the falling down, but the staying down.

508. Our business in the world is not to succeed, but to continue to fail in good spirits.
Robert Louis Stevenson

509. Better to attempt something great and fail than to attempt something small and succeed.

FAITH

510. Believing is as much an integral factor in man as are eating and sleeping. He neither gains nor loses faith; he merely changes the object of it. . . . Man is simply an inveterate, incurable, inevitable believer.
Samuel Miller

511. The opposite of sin is not virtue but faith.
Soren Kierkegaard

512. God does not expect us to submit our faith to him without reason, but the very limits of reason make faith a necessity.

Saint Augustine

513. If life is a comedy to him who thinks, and a tragedy to him who feels, it is a victory to him who believes.

514. Faith sees the invisible, believes the incredible, and receives the impossible.

515. For all that has been—thanks! To all that shall be—yes!

Dag Hammarskjold

516. Historical facts never create faith, only faith creates faith.

John Macquarrie

517. What we need is a faith that can open up the future and be stronger than death.

518. Doubt sees the wall;
Faith sees the way.
Doubt sees the darkest night;
Faith sees the day.
Doubt dreads to take a step;
Faith soars high.
Doubt questions who believes;
Faith answers, "I."

519. Without Christ, not one step; with Him, anywhere!

David Livingstone

520. Faith does not wish, hope, or desire—faith receives.

Ord Morrow

521. Faith is that belief of the intellect, consent of the affections, and act of the will by which the soul places itself in the keeping of Christ as its ruler and Savior.

Daniel Whedon

522. Our faith is so much faith that we have to have faith even in our faith.

Karl Barth

523. Faith is not jumping to conclusions. It is concluding to jump.

W. T. Purkiser

524. Faith is the abandonment of man's own security

and the readiness to find security only in the unseen beyond in God.

Rudolf Bultmann

525. Paul's letters have two main sections. One deals with doctrine—the believing side of faith. The other section deals with conduct—the behaving side of faith.

W. T. Purkiser

526. Seek not to understand that you may believe, but rather believe that you may understand.

Saint Augustine

527. Belief is truth held in the mind; faith is fire in the heart.

Joseph F. Newton

528. The disease with which the human mind now labors is want of faith.

Ralph Waldo Emerson

529. Faith is the capacity to trust God while not being able to make sense out of everything.

James Kok

(See also: Trust.)

FAITHFULNESS

530. If we are correct and right in our Christian life at every point, but refuse to stand for the truth at a particular point where the battle rages—then we are traitors to Christ.

Martin Luther

531. This above all: to thine own self be true.
And it must follow, as the night the day,
Thou canst not then be false to any man.

William Shakespeare

532. The final criterion that will be used by God to judge us is not success but faithfulness.

533. One day every man will have his reward, and it will be based not on the greatness of his task, but on his faithfulness.

M. P. Horban

THE FAMILY

534. The family circle is the supreme conductor of Christianity.

Henry Drummond

535. Loving relationships are a family's best protection against the challenges of the world.

Bernie Wiebe

536. The number of hours which husband and wife are able to spend alone with each other, or which father or mother is able to spend with the children, may be much less important than what goes on during those hours in terms of the richness and quality of the interpersonal relationship involved.

537. A family watching television is a way of doing nothing together.

538. There is never much trouble in any family where the children hope someday to resemble their parents.

William Lyon Phelps

539. Considering the number of divorces today, it seems that more parents are running away from home than children.

(See also: Christian Home; Marriage, Parenthood.)

FANATICISM

540. A fanatic is one who can't change his mind and won't change the subject.

541. A fanatic is a person who redoubles his efforts when he has lost his objectives.

FATHERHOOD

542. It is sobering to recall that fathers bear the title God Himself has chosen as a picture of His relationship to His people.

543. I [should have spent] more time with my children, especially my two sons, when they were little. You have to get with your children when they're real little. I didn't know that. I thought I'd get with them when they got to be teens, but then it's too late.

Billy Graham

544. He that will have his son have a respect for him and his orders, must himself have a great reverence for his son.

John Locke

FEAR

545. Men who fear God face life fearlessly. Men who do not fear God end up fearing everything.

Richard C. Halverson

546. It is only the fear of God that can deliver us from the fear of man.

John Witherspoon

(See also: Peace of Mind.)

FINANCES

547. The surest way to establish your credit is to work so hard that you don't need it.

548. One benefit of higher prices is it doesn't leave you with enough money to buy the things you don't need.

549. Americans often spend more than they make on things they don't need to impress people they don't like.

550. To compute the cost of living, simply take your income and add 20 per cent.

FLATTERY

551. Flatterers look like friends as wolves look like dogs.

George Chapman

FOLLY

552. The wise learn from tragedy; the foolish merely repeat it.

Michael Novak

553. The continuous toleration of error inevitably leads to the surrender of faith.

554. There is no surer guarantee of trouble than the combination of enthusiasm and ignorance.

555. What a silly fellow must be he who would do the Devil's work for nothing.

Joseph Andrews

556. Lustful ambition breeds the fools who bid for counterfeit kingdoms. From such preserve us, Good Lord.

Richard John Neuhaus

557.   Man is pretty much a fool—
       When it's hot he wants it cool,
       When it's cool he wants it hot,
       Always wanting what it's not.

558. Men have a real capacity for kidding themselves. Doctors of philosophy often become doctors of "foolosophy" and never sense the difference.

Chester E. Tulga

559. Nothing undermines authority like foolish rules.
Edward Wakin

FOOD SUPPLY

560. Statisticians tell us that while you're eating dinner tonight, 417 people will die of starvation.

FORGIVENESS

561. The only true forgiveness is that which is offered and extended even before the offender has apologized and sought it.
Soren Kierkegaard

562. In forgiveness, you bear your own anger and wrath at the sin of another, voluntarily accepting responsibility for the hurt he has inflicted upon you.
David Augsburger

563. Guilt too long unforgiven may become "unforgivable." For the guilt-ridden person, death finally becomes an easier option than confession. Forgiveness is the most difficult thing in the world to accept. Why? It requires the honest acceptance of our own inability to save ourselves. Accepting forgiveness is tantamount to absolute self-debasement while wholely leaning on the grace of the forgiver.

(See also: God's Forgiveness.)

FREEDOM

564. It is impossible to mentally or socially enslave a Bible-reading people.
Horace Greeley

565. What is it that the gentlemen wish? What would they have? Is life so dear or peace so sweet as to be purchased at the price of chains and slavery? Forbid it, Almighty God! I know not what course others may take, but as for me, give me liberty or give me death.
Patrick Henry

566. Absolute freedom is absolute nonsense.
D. Elton Trueblood

567. The greatest glory of a free-born people is to transmit that freedom to their children.
William C. Havard

568. The most stringent protection of free speech

would not protect a man who falsely shouts "fire" in a crowded theatre causing panic and injury.

Oliver Wendell Holmes

569. More freedom is acquired only by the right use of the freedom we do have.

570. To be free from responsibility is to be prisoner to a conspiracy of hazards. This makes you as free as a drifting balloon or a driverless car.

571. Inequality exists as long as liberty exists. It unavoidably results from that very liberty itself.

Alexander Hamilton

572. The value of freedom cannot be appraised apart from either its discipline or its dissipation. And, however much this basic difference may vary by degree, all of man's problems—both collective and individual—are symptomatic of the eternally irreconcilable difference between a freedom sanctified by discipline and that which is seduced by desire.

573. Freedom! No word was ever spoken that has held greater hope, demanded greater sacrifice, needed more to be nurtured, blessed more the giver ... or came closer to being God's will on earth.

Omar N. Bradley

574. Total freedom is total emptiness.

575. If I were not a willing slave to Christ, what could I do with freedom?

Virginia S. Horton

576. It is by the goodness of God that in our country we have three unspeakably precious things: freedom of speech, freedom of conscience, and the prudence never to practice either of them.

Mark Twain

577. True liberty is being free to do what one ought to do; false liberty is feeling free to do what one wants to do.

George E. Failing

578. Extremism which we see today in the arts, in custom, in morals, in religion, in dress and in relations between the sexes is all practiced in the name of freedom. But this extremism is the harbinger of tyranny which is even now hacking away at the foundations of our republic.

FRIENDSHIP

579. You make more friends by becoming interested in other people than by trying to interest other people in yourself.

Dale Carnegie

580. No one can develop freely in this world and find a full life without feeling understood by at least one person.

Paul Tournier

581. Better to have a forthright enemy than an untrustworthy friend.

582. Go oft to the house of thy friend, for weeds choke the unused path.

Ralph Waldo Emerson

583. Against a foe I can myself defend,
But Heaven protect me from a blundering friend.
D. W. Thompson

584. To lose a friend is the greatest of all evils.

Seneca

(See also: Interpersonal Relations.)

FULFILLMENT

585. The man who never covets never suffers from unfulfillment—either real or imagined.

586. The fulfillment of climbing is not to be compared with the thrills of sliding. But the greatest thrill follows the hard trek to the top while the greatest unfulfillment comes at the end of a long though thrilling slide.

587. If one has all the world without the Savior, he is poverty stricken; while if in possession of nothing else in all the world save Christ, he is totally satisfied.

(See also: Contentment.)

THE FUTURE

588. If you do not think about the future, you cannot have one.

John Galsworthy

(See also: The New Year.)

G

GAMBLING

589. Overheard in Las Vegas: "I came here in a ten thousand dollar Cadillac; now I'm going home in a forty thousand dollar bus."

GENERATION GAP

590. Christ does not bridge the generation gap. He bridges the regeneration gap, and when he does, the resulting reconciliation leaves no gaps at all.

GLUTTONY

591. There is something incongruous about asking God to bless buttered rolls and pecan pie at 10:30 P.M. when none of us need them.

LaVerna Klippenstein

592. Many a man has dug his own grave with his teeth.

GOD

593. The hardness of God is kinder than the softness of men, and His compulsion is our liberation.

C. S. Lewis

594. Those who deny the existence of God are hard put to explain the existence of man.

Harold Berry

595. The person who is separated from God is necessarily also separated from his own best interest.

596. God whispers in our pleasures but shouts in our pains.

C. S. Lewis

597. A possibility is a hint from God.

Soren Kierkegaard

598. God's will is not an itinerary but an attitude.

Andrew Dhuse

599. Bertrand Russell, an avowed and militant atheist, wrote in his autobiography: "The centre of me is always and eternally a terrible pain—a curious wild pain—a searching for something beyond what the world contains, something transfigured and infinite—the beatific vision—God—I do not find it, I do not think it is to be found—but the love of it is my life—it's like passionate love for a ghost."

600. The world needs a creator not only for its beginning but for every moment of its being.

Robert F. Capon

601. Nationalism is concerned with the nation and socialism with the class. Only God makes a private visit with the individual.

William James

602. The proper study of a Christian is the Godhead. The highest science, the loftiest speculation, the mightiest philosophy which can ever engage the attention of a child of God is the name, the person, the work, the doings and the existence of the Great God whom he calls his Father.

Charles Spurgeon

603. If there were no God it would be necessary to invent him.

Voltaire

604. A man can no more diminish God's glory by refusing to worship Him than a lunatic can put out the sun by scribbling the word "darkness" on the walls of his cell.

C. S. Lewis

605. Truth forever on the scaffold,
Wrong forever on the throne;
Yet that scaffold sways the future,
And behind the dim unknown
Standeth God within the shadows,
Keeping watch above his own.

James Russell Lowell

GOD'S FORGIVENESS

606. God's love is crucified by your own sin—crucified but not destroyed. Once we come to really see what our sin does to the innocent Christ, the immediate choice of being sorry or selfish is thrust upon us. The great miracle in the economy of God awaits the contrite heart—it

is the life-giving redemptive miracle of forgiveness. The Christian life is paradise because God's forgiveness removes the burden of guilt and adds the promise of eternal life.

GOD'S JUDGMENT

607. We love to play on the silver trumpet of grace rather than on the ram's horn of justice.

Charles Spurgeon

608. In *Summer of the Red Wolf* by Morris L. West, Hannah says: "We all love the preacher who has heaven in his hand and who says not a word about the other place." But the same Jesus who said gently: "Consider the lilies of the field"; also thundered: "Except ye repent, ye shall all likewise perish."

609. Though the mills of God grind slowly,
Yet they grind exceeding small;
Though with patience He stands waiting,
With exactness grinds He all.

Henry Wadsworth Longfellow

610. Better to meet the Lord before you die in grace, than after you die in judgment.

611. In the day when all men will stand before God, the significant question for each of us will no longer be what we think of Christ, but what He thinks of us.

Elva J. Hoover

612. God has already set a time when we shall be in His hands. What He does with us then depends on what we do with Him now.

Bonnie Kile

GOD'S LOVE

613. The only way God's love makes sense is when it is seen as personal [not mechanical]. He doesn't start your stalled car for you; but He comes and sits with you in the snow bank.

Robert F. Capon

614. God does not love us because we are valuable. We are valuable because God loves us.

Fulton J. Sheen

615. If God takes your lump of clay and remolds it, it will be on the basis of love and not on the basis of power over you.

James Conway

616. The truth about man is that he needs to be loved the most when he deserves it the least. Only God can fulfill this incredible need. Only God can provide a love so deep it saves from the depths.

617. The love of Christ converts unsuspected potentialities into unbelievable actualities.

Paul S. Rees

GOD'S SOVEREIGNTY

618. If you think you see the ark of the Lord falling, you can be sure it is due to a swimming in your head.

John Newton

619. I have lived a long time, sir, and the longer I live the more convincing proofs I see of this truth—that God governs in the affairs of men.

Benjamin Franklin

GOD'S WILL

620. God does not will every circumstance; but He does have a will in every circumstance.

J. Kenneth Grider

(See also: Divine Guidance.)

GOOD FRIDAY THEME

621. Men will always crucify Christ because His presence exposes their sin. Covered sin causes guilt. Exposed sin adds shame. Man can live with guilt through suppression and compensation. But open shame is unbearable. The men who crucified Christ supposed they could get rid of their shame if they could banish the Christ who exposed their sin and "caused" their shame.

622. The concept of resurrection is welcomed by all; but the necessary, prior concern of self-crucifixion is a higher price than most men are willing to pay.

623. The persecutors of Christ challenged Him: "Come down from the Cross and we will believe in you." But William Booth has wisely pointed out that it is precisely because Jesus did not come down from the Cross that we believe in Him.

(See also: Lenten Theme; Self Denial.)

GOSSIP

(See Censoriousness.)

GRACE

624. Free grace! But hurry! The offer may expire soon.

625. Man is born broken; he lives by mending. The grace of God is the glue.

Eugene O'Neil

626. Grace is God's all for your bankruptcy.

Torrey Johnson

(See also: God's Love.)

GREATNESS

627. The greatest among men is always ready to serve and yet is unconscious of the service.

Helena P. Blavatsky

GUILT

628. One of the most distressing signs of contemporary times is the denial of guilt.

Fulton J. Sheen

629. Virtue is its own reward, the significant part of which is freedom from guilt; and sin is self-punishing, the significant part of which is the cutting edge of guilt.

630. It is a consoling idea that before God we are always in the wrong.

Soren Kierkegaard

631. Guilt may be defined as being ashamed to live and afraid to die.

632. Guilt too long unforgiven may become "unforgivable." For the guilt-ridden person, death finally becomes an easier option than confession.

633. We cannot bear the company of those we crucify.

John Lewis Gilmore

H

HAPPINESS

634. The consideration that human happiness and moral duty are inseparably connected will always continue to prompt me to promote the former by inculcating the practice of the latter.

George Washington

635. One of Satan's biggest lies is the claim that sin adds to human happiness. If this were true then the greatest sinners would be the happiest people. But the very reverse is the case.

W. T. Purkiser

636. America has more things than any other nation in the world, and more books on how to find happiness.

W. E. Sangster

637. Existence is a strange bargain. Life owes us little and we owe it everything. The only true happiness comes from squandering ourselves for a purpose.

John Mason Brown

638. Man has traversed the globe, orbited the earth, split the atom, created electronic brains, and transplanted hearts; yet he is unhappy and unfilled.

639. It is possible to divide the world of happiness-hunters into two classes—those who seek happiness by "getting" and those who seek it by "giving."

Charles F. Potter

640. When we forget the big dimension of our nature ... trying [only] to satisfy one part of us at the expense of the rest of us, we end up with small temporary pleasures, but not happiness.

J. Wallace Hamilton

641. Happiness is being holy to the Lord and helpful to men.

George Gritter

642. The United States Constitution doesn't guarantee happiness, only the pursuit of it. You have to catch up with it yourself.

Benjamin Franklin

643. Time will convince even the blindest and most frivolous of us that happiness is no more to be found in the places we usually look, than it is to be dug out of the earth. But the man who knows the secret of prayer lives at the top of human happiness.

William Law

644. Happiness is the fulfillment of the total self. The pleasure seeker is usually an unhappy person because his search and his find are relevant only to a part of himself, while much of his "total self" goes unfilled.

645. Happiness is grace, not works; a fringe benefit, not salary.

Eldon Weisheit

646. It isn't our position but our disposition that makes us happy.

647. The only happiness that will last is a happiness which is not dependent on things, or circumstances, or other people. Such happiness comes only through knowing Christ as Savior and Lord.

648. The strength and the happiness of a man consists in finding out the way in which God is going, and going in that way too.

Henry Ward Beecher

649. Searching for true happiness in the context of a godless life is like looking for a needle in a haystack that doesn't have any.

W. T. Purkiser

650. Happiness is neither within us or without; it is the union of ourselves with God.

651. Fulfillment is found through sacrifice, hope through service, and victory through suffering.

652. We try to be our own masters as if we had created ourselves. Then we hopelessly strive to invent some sort of happiness for ourselves outside of God, apart from God. And out of that hopeless attempt has come nearly all that we call human history . . . the long terrible story of man trying to find something other than God which will make him happy.

C. S. Lewis

653. The plain fact is we aren't made for a sense of well-being that rises or falls with what we can get our hands on. We are made for whatever God brings to pass out of the hard soil of struggle, out of the creative effort of our souls.

Arnold G. Kuntz

(See also: Contentment.)

HATE

654. Hating people is like burning down your house to get rid of a rat.

Harry Emerson Fosdick

655. To have an unforgiving spirit is to burn a bridge over which you may someday want to travel.

656. Nothing angers a man more than to be discovered in his hatred by love.

HEALTH

657. Many a man has dug his own grave with his teeth.

658. If you want to live twice as long: eat half as much, sleep twice as much, drink (water) three times as much and laugh four times as much.

John H. Cable

(See also: Gluttony.)

HEAVEN

659. Hell is where everyone is doing his own thing. Paradise is where everyone is doing God's thing.

Thomas Howard

660. Joy is the serious business of heaven.

C. S. Lewis

HEDONISM

(See: Materialism and Hedonism.)

HELL

661. The only thing which makes the church uniquely relevant is hell.

662. How hot is hell? If you piled up all the timber in Maine, put on this timber all the coal in Pennsylvania, and poured on this coal and timber all the oil in Oklahoma, and set it all on fire and waited until it was burning its worst, then took a man out of hell and threw him into the midst of it, he would just naturally freeze to death.

663. I wouldn't pay a nickel to a preacher who did not preach on hell enough to keep my children afraid of going there.

Seth Rees

664. Hell is where everyone is doing his own thing. Paradise is where everyone is doing God's thing.

Thomas Howard

665. If there is no hell, there is no good news. If there is no hell, the Bible has no relevance. If there is no hell, atonement for sin is as unintelligent as it is unnecessary.

666. The old-time evangelists used to stress the tragedy of men and women individually going to hell. We don't hear very much about that nowadays, because they say people don't believe in hell, but I notice they talk a lot about it in their conversations.

Peter Marshall

667. When hell drops out of religion, order drops out of society.

668. Preaching on hell and judgment brings conviction, not because it scares people, but because it is raw spiritual truth which the Holy Spirit can use to convict men of unrepented sin.

669. Ungodly people who have no fear of hell use the word profanely, but hell is nothing to laugh about and they will not be laughing when they get there.

J. Hershey Longenecker

HISTORY

670. No one is free from the history he has inherited.
Willy Brandt

671. History is the history of liberty and liberty is the eternal creator of history and itself the subject of every history.

Benedetto Croce

672. Those who cannot remember the past are condemned to repeat it.

George Santayana

673. It is interesting that if you read the introduction to almost any history book, no matter what century, it will describe the time as one of "great upheaval." So, if we review our history, we find that we of the twentieth century are experiencing what nearly every other century has also experienced—great upheaval.

This is not to underestimate the seriousness of our situation. Just because other centuries have had their problems, we cannot simply shrug and say, "O well, things will sort themselves out, eventually." The simple but stark truth is: things just do not sort themselves out. The graveyards are full of soldiers and innocent bystanders who, far from living through their crises, were crushed by them. The Babylonian order crumbled before the Greek, the Greek before the Roman, the Roman before the Gothic. The Saxon order fell before the Norman. The Catholic order fell before the Reformation. The Religious order fell before the Enlightenment. Things just don't sort themselves out; they are blasted.

HOLINESS

674. A true test of holiness is whether it fills one with an overwhelming concern for unholy people.

675. Even if it is only a game, I would still rather enjoy the holy life than live a supposedly more honest life of grim and senseless boredom.

Blaise Pascal

HOLY SPIRIT

676. Men ablaze are invincible. For fifty days the facts of the Gospel were complete, but no conversions were recorded. Pentecost registered three thousand the first day.

Samuel Chadwick

677. The Holy Spirit expects us to take seriously the answers He has already provided, the light He has already shed; and He does not expect us to plead for things that have already been denied.

Paul Little

678. I do not find in the Old Testament or in the New Testament, neither in Christian biography, in church history or in personal Christian testimonies the experience of any person who was ever filled with the Holy Ghost and who didn't know it.

A. W. Tozer

HOPE

679. You are surprised that the world is losing its grip and full of pressing tribulations? Do not hold onto the old man, the world; do not refuse to regain your youth

in Christ who says to you: "The world is passing away, the world is short of breath. Do not fear; thy youth shall be renewed as an eagle."

Saint Augustine

680. Everything that is done in the world is done by hope.

Martin Luther

681. Hope is itself a species of happiness, and, perhaps, the chief happiness which the world affords.

Samuel Johnson

682. If joy is coming, hope will have proved itself right; if disaster, hope will have strengthened us to meet it.

Ardis Whitman

683. Other men see only a hopeless end, but the Christian rejoices in an endless hope.

Gilbert M. Beeken

684. The future belongs to those who belong to God. This is hope.

W. T. Purkiser

HUMANISM

685. It is vain, O men, that you seek within yourselves the cure for your miseries. Your principal maladies are pride, which cuts off from God, and sensuality, which binds you to the earth. Either you imagine you are gods yourselves, or, if you grasp the vanity of such a pretention, you are cast into the other abyss, and suppose yourselves to be like the beasts of the field and seek your good in carnality.

Blaise Pascal

686. If it is unreasonable to hold a religious faith that cannot be demonstrated, surely it is irrational to defend a humanistic faith that the evidence so universally contradicts.

Langdon Gilkey

687. Humanism is not wrong in its cry for sociological healing, but humanism is not producing it.

Francis A. Schaeffer

688. What worldly-wise men presume to be the best of human potentialities are often projected onto God in what is often called Christian humanism. Thus, man creates God in his own image. But man's concepts of his best self and the attributes of God have no necessary relationship, and no Biblical basis in fact. The worldling's best self—the humanistic ideal—rules out the total

sinfulness of man, but the Bible doesn't. The humanistic ideal rules out moral absolutes, but the Bible doesn't. The humanistic ideal rules out hell, but the Bible doesn't.

HUMILITY

689. He is made more worthy who dispenses with what he deserves.

690. Experienced mountain climbers report that the best way to take advantage of the breathtaking view at the mountain top is to stay on your knees. This is to avoid being blown over by the strong winds present on mountain peaks. Thus it is with life. Once we climb to a pinnacle of success, we would do well to remain on our knees—to avoid being blown off the peak.

Peggy Wells

691. God does not want us to think less of ourselves. He wants us not to think of ourselves at all.

Andrew Dhuse

692. Life is a long lesson in humility.

James S. Barrie

693. You can do anything you want to if you don't care who gets the credit for it.

Lillian Dickson

694. The only wisdom we can hope to acquire is the wisdom of humility—humility is endless.

T. S. Eliot

695. We wouldn't worry so much about what other people thought of us if we knew how seldom they did.

696. Man is never so tall as when he kneels before God—never so great as when he humbles himself before God. And the man who kneels to God can stand up to anything.

Louis H. Evans

697. To contend for the faith in humility is one of the hardest tasks for the committed believer.

Cyrus N. Nelson

698. God giveth grace to the humble. When we try to avoid being humbled, we are avoiding a means of grace.

HUMOR

699. Humor will never destroy anything that is genuine. All it can do is puncture balloons.

Kenneth L. Wilson

HYPOCRISY

700. Our prayers for the evangelization of the world are only bitter irony so long as we only give our lip service and draw back from the sacrifice of ourselves.

701. The church without power is a factory for hypocrites.

Samuel M. Shoemaker

702. If fool there be then I am he,
To claim another I than me.
For I am all the I I see,
The only I that I can be.

703. The church spends too much of its time trying to make non-Christians act like Christians.

L. Nelson Bell

704. Pretending is so characteristic of the modern style of life. In fact we seem to have a thing about revealing our bodies and concealing our spirits.

705. The worst lies are those that most resemble the truth.

706. A failure to live one's self-consciousness is a kind of living death.

707. There is that which is more contrary to Christianity than heresy or any schism, and that is to play religion.

Soren Kierkegaard

708. The person who leads a double life often gets through it in half the time.

709. How can young people believe very much in our Christianity if after we serve them up a goodly helping of Christian theory, we persist in living so much like the unregenerate?

710. Spiritual cheapness and triviality does more harm, when displayed by those professing to be spiritual, than all the demons of unbelief.

Walter Wagoner

711. The world's greatest fool is the person who participates in the church but rejects Jesus Christ.

I

IMMORALITY

712. The path of least resistance is what makes both men and rivers crooked.

713. Every individual or national degeneration is immediately revealed by a directly proportional degeneration in language.

Joseph de Maistre

714. What were once vices are now the manners of the day.

Seneca

715. Our difficulty is not from the breaking of moral laws, but from the rejection of any moral law at all.

Will Herberg

716. The problem is not necessarily X-rated movies; the problem is X-rated minds.

Raymond C. Wilson

(See also: Dishonesty; United States—Moral Climate.)

IMMORTALITY

717. Some morning you will pick up the paper and read that D. L. Moody is dead. When you do, don't believe it. For at that very moment I will be more alive than I am now.

Dwight L. Moody

718. Nature does not know extinction. All that it knows is transformation. . . . Everything that science has taught me—and continues to teach me—strengthens my belief in the continuity of our spiritual existence after death.

Wernher Von Braun

INFLUENCE

719. When I think of those who have influenced my life the most, I think not of the great but of the good.
John Knox

720. There is no power on earth that can neutralize the influence of a high, pure, simple, and useful life.
Booker T. Washington

721. Example is not the main thing in influencing others—it is the only thing.
Albert Schweitzer

722. We Christians have never been the whole bolt of cloth—always just a remnant. We have never been the loaf of bread—only the leaven. We have never been the side of meat—only the salt. But as leaven lifts the loaf and as salt preserves the meat so the Christian community has before it the challenge to influence the degenerate society in which it exists.

INTEGRITY

723. For when the One Great Scorer comes
To write against your name,
He writes—not that you won or lost,
But how you played the game.
Grantland Rice

724. This above all: to thine own self be true.
And it must follow as the night the day,
Thou canst not then be false to any man.
William Shakespeare

725. If the deal isn't good for the other party, it isn't good for you.
B. C. Forbes

726. Parents should tell their children that failing every subject with integrity is more to be preferred than to get straight As and cheat only once in the process.

727. On the eve of George Washington's inauguration he said: "Integrity and firmness are all I can promise."

728. Without integrity, there is no freedom. With integrity, freedom will not become license.

(See also: Character.)

INTELLECTUALISM

729. When, O when, will American intellectuals learn

that self-righteous moralism is but one step away from tyranny?

Andrew M. Greeley

730. An intellectual is a person who puts a high premium on thinking but an even higher one on thoughtfulness.

Nathan M. Pusey

INTERNATIONAL RELATIONS

731. A neutral nation is usually one,
(And brother, it's not funny)
Which always takes the Russian's side,
And also U.S. money.

F. G. Kernan

INTERPERSONAL RELATIONS

732. [Authentic Christian experience] doesn't make things easier, in fact, in a way it makes them harder because it cuts out self-pity and refuses the refuge of resentment and revenge.

Rosemary Haughton

733. The only people with whom you should try to get even are those who have helped you.

Mae Maloo

734. Two great talkers will not travel far together.

George Borrow

735. Flatterers look like friends as wolves look like dogs.

George Chapman

736. A good listener is popular everywhere. Not only that, but after a while he knows something too.

737. You make more friends by becoming interested in other people than by trying to interest other people in yourself.

Dale Carnegie

738. To dwell there above,
With the saints that we love—
That will be glory.
But to dwell here below,
With the saints that we know—
That's another story!

Henry R. Brandt

739. When we are in tune with Christ we are in harmony with each other.

Vance Havner

740. When at a loss for the right thing to say, try silence.

741. I don't know any strangers, just friends I haven't met.

Jennie Grossinger

742. In necessary things, unity; in doubtful things, liberty; in all things, charity.

Saint Augustine

743. Instead of giving advice, ask for some. Instead of testing all actions against their possible effects on you, test them against understanding the needs of others.

Jean Alexander

INVOLVEMENT

744. True godliness does not turn men out of the world, but enables them to live better in it, and excites their endeavors to mend it.

William Penn

745. Even if you are on the right track, you will get run over if you just sit there.

Bennie Bargen

746. What good is "peace of mind" if we lie down and sleep while the world goes to hell?

Billy Graham

747. If we are correct and right in our Christian life at every point, but refuse to stand for the truth at a particular point where the battle rages—then we are traitors to Christ.

Martin Luther

(See also: Christian Action.)

J

JESUS CHRIST

748. If you wish to be disappointed, look to others. If you wish to be downhearted, look to yourself. If you wish to be encouraged . . . look upon Jesus Christ.
Erich Sauer

749. The most outstanding record that is graven on the scroll of time is the date of the birth of Jesus Christ. No issued document is legal, no signed check is valid, and no business receipt is of value unless it bears the statistical reference to this great historic event.
Homer G. Rhea, Jr.

750. He who has nothing to say about Jesus Christ, has nothing to say.
Henk Vigeveno

751. Assuming the divinity of Jesus Christ, how could you doubt His virgin birth? But assuming the humanity of Jesus only, how could you believe it?
Ben Haden

752. The Greeks said that the ends of life are three: the good, the true, and the beautiful. The Hindus said the means of life are also three in number: the way of knowledge, the way of devotion, and the way of deeds. But Jesus Christ tells us that He is both the means and the end: "I am the way, the truth, and the life." In other words, God in Christ is universal beauty become a picture, universal goodness become a life, and universal truth become an invincible Lord.

753. Christ is the still point of the turning world.
T. S. Eliot

754. In light of the rejection by men of Christ, Francis of Assisi once exclaimed: "Love is not loved!"

755. The name of Christ excludes all merit of our own.
John Calvin

756. Nineteen wide centuries have come and gone and today Christ is the centerpiece of the human race and the leader of progress. All the armies that ever marched, and all the navies that ever were built, and all the parliaments that ever sat and all the kings that ever reigned—all of these put together have not affected the life of man upon this earth as powerfully as has that one solitary life.

757. If Jesus Christ were not virgin born, then, of course, He had a human father; if He had a human father, then He inherited the nature of the father; as that father had a nature of sin, then He inherited his nature of sin; then Jesus Himself was a lost sinner and He Himself needed a Savior from sin. Deny the virgin birth of Jesus Christ and you paralyze the whole scheme of redemption by Jesus Christ.

I. M. Haldeman

758. Many things have the appearance of excellence, but the knowledge of Christ surpasses everything.

John Calvin

(See also: Second Coming of Christ.)

JOY

759. Joy is the serious business of heaven.

C. S. Lewis

760. If doing God's will is all that counts for you, then no matter what the rest of life brings, you can find joy.

Vernon C. Lyons

761. Joy is the royal standard floating from the flagstaff telling us that the King is in residence within.

762. Joy is never in our power, and pleasure is. I doubt whether anyone who has tasted joy would ever, if both were in his power, exchange it for all the pleasure in the world.

C. S. Lewis

763. Grief can take care of itself; but to get the full value of joy, you must have somebody to share it with.

Mark Twain

K

KINDNESS

764. Life is mostly froth and bubbles;
Only two things stand like stone:
Kindness in another's troubles,
Courage in your own.

765. Manners are of more importance than laws. Upon them, in a great measure, the laws depend. The law can touch us here and there, now and then. Manners are what vex or soothe, corrupt or purify, exalt or debase, barbarize or refine, by a constant, steady, uniform and insensible operation, like that of the air we breathe in. They give their whole form and color to our lives. According to their quality, they aid morals, they supply them, or they totally destroy them.

Edmund Burke

766. When you call in the woods, the echo returns. A similar thing happens to the person who exercises courtesy.

767. Be kind; everyone you meet is fighting a hard battle.

John Watson

768. Kind words can never die. But without kind deeds they can sound mighty sick.

769. The greatest thing a man can do for his Heavenly Father is to be kind to some of His other children.

Henry Drummond

KNOWLEDGE

770. Knowledge is power only if a man knows which facts not to bother about.

Robert Lynd

771. Some students drink at the fountain of knowledge; others just gargle.

772. Knowledge is folly unless grace is her guide.

L

LABOR

773. Good for the body is the work of the body, and good for the soul is the work of the soul, and good for either is the work of the other.

Henry David Thoreau

774. Too much idleness, I have observed, fills up a man's time much more completely, and leaves him less his own master, than any sort of employment whatsoever.

Edmund Burke

775. If this country is ever demoralized it will come from trying to live without work.

Abraham Lincoln

776. Here's a stubborn truth
On which you can bet:
The harder you work,
The luckier you get.

L. J. Huber

777. A worker who does only what he has to do is a slave. One who willingly does more than is required of him is a free man.

778. A stranger came to three workmen, all employed on the same job. He asked each worker what he was doing. Growled the first man: "I'm breaking rocks." Said the second: "I'm earning a living." But the third man replied with a smile: "I'm building a cathedral."

Sir Christopher Wren

779. One machine can now do the work of one hundred ordinary men, but no machine can do the work of one extraordinary man.

780. A man can do only what he can do. But if he does that each day he can sleep at night and do it again the next day.
Albert Schweitzer

781. Although it may seem
That the process is slow,
Still, work is the yeast
That raises the dough.
Mary Hamlett Goodman

782. O Lord, Thou givest us everything at the price of an effort.
Leonardo da Vinci

783. At the workingman's house hunger looks in, but dare not enter.
Benjamin Franklin

784. No nation can prosper till it learns that there is as much dignity in tilling a field as in writing a poem.
Booker T. Washington

785. There is no substitute for hard work.
Thomas Alva Edison

786. A society in which the average person is trying to get all that he can while he performs the least possible service is already sick unto death.
D. Elton Trueblood

LAW ENFORCEMENT

787. Guns for the criminal,
Gloves for the cop,
Makes a society
That soon will go "pop."
But guns for the cop,
Support for him too,
Makes a society
For the good and the true.

LEADERSHIP

788. On the eve of his inauguration George Washington said: "Integrity and firmness are all I can promise."

LEGALISM

789. "We don't smoke, and we don't chew, and we don't run with folks that do." But Jesus did run with them sometimes. We tend to avoid people who appear evil, rather than the appearance of evil.

LENTEN THEME

790. So long as Jesus was misunderstood He was followed by the crowd. When they came to really understand Him, they crucified Him.

Dan Harman

(See also: Good Friday Theme; Self-Denial.)

LIBERALISM

791. To the modern liberal mind, discipline has an almost pornographic sound. But discipline is necessary to freedom.

Donald Barr

792. The contemporary church is often guilty of throwing away the Gift while holding in high esteem the superficial wrappings.

793. A liberal is one who transforms Biblical terms into theological bubble gum, and who blows bubbles like a child show-off.

794. The only thing liberals want to conserve is the air they breathe—nearly everything else, such as law, order, and disciplined freedom are expendable.

795. The modern church has become obsessed with a patented "cure-all" mentality that mixes Marx, Freud, Camus, Sartre, Bultmann, Marcuse and Jesus into one incomprehensible blob.

Leslie H. Woodson

796. Richard Niebuhr's devastating indictment of liberal theology: "A God without wrath brought men without sin into a Kingdom without judgment through Christ without a cross."

(See also: Social Gospel.)

LIBERATION

797. Every movement which claims to be a liberating force is not. Real liberation is freedom from sin, guilt, and fear; and is ironically to be found, not in some vague ideal called Christian freedom, but only in the decision to choose the loving Christ as the Master to whom you will willingly and eagerly be a slave, and from whom you must always refuse to be liberated. The only way to sufficiently shun wrong masters is to always serve the right One.

(See also: Christian Life; Freedom.)

LIFE

798. We are shaped and fashioned by what we love.
Johann Wolfgang Goethe

799. Lives based on "having" are less free than lives based either on "doing" or on "being."
William James

800. We make a living by what we get—a life by what we give.

801. There are two tragedies in life. One is not to get your heart's desire and the other is to get it.
George Bernard Shaw

802. What I believe about God is the most important thing about me.
A. W. Tozer

803. Where you go hereafter depends on what you go after here.
W. T. Purkiser

804. The two greatest days in a person's life are the day he was born and the day he finds out why he was born.

805. Equality is a quantitative term and, therefore, love knows nothing of it. Authority exercised with humility, and obedience accepted with delight are the very lines along which our spirits live.
C. S. Lewis

806. Life consists not in holding good cards, but in playing those you do hold well.
Josh Billings

807. The greatest question of our time is not communism vs. individualism, not Europe versus America nor East versus West. It is whether man can bear to live without God.
Will Durant

808. Philosophy theorizes about life. Psychology analyzes life. History records life. Sociology classifies life. All men desire life. But Jesus said: "I am the Life."

809. The person who is separated from God is necessarily also separated from his own best interest.

810. If life is a comedy to him who thinks, and a tragedy to him who feels, it is a victory to him who believes.

811. Every act rewards itself.
Ralph Waldo Emerson

812. Only those who plan for death are really prepared for life.

813. Most of us would get along very well if we used the advice we give to others.

814. In life, as in golf, sincerity and hard work are not substitutes for heading in the right direction.

815. The greatest waste in the world is the difference between what we are and what we could be.
Ben Herbster

816. You're as young as your faith and as old as your despair.
Willie Vest

817. Scoring bull's eyes in life takes more skill than simply shooting holes and drawing rings around them.
William P. Seibert

818. Life can only be understood backwards, however, it must be lived forwards.
Soren Kierkegaard

819. There are three things that confront every man: life, death, and eternity.

820. Fear not that thy life shall come to an end, but rather that it shall never have a beginning.
Cardinal Newman

821. Life offers only two alternatives: crucifixion with Christ or self-destruction without Him.

822. The moving finger writes,
And having writ moves on;
Nor all your piety, nor wit
Can cancel half a line of it.
Omar Khayyam

823. Most men live lives of quiet desperation.
Henry David Thoreau

824. We are not free to cease being free.
Jean Paul Sartre

825. Life is what is happening to you while you're making other plans.

826. Life is a mirror: if you frown at it, it frowns back; if you smile, it returns the greeting.
William M. Thackeray

827. All the world is a hospital and everyone in it a terminal patient.

828. Those who opt for life on any terms have never known life in its fullest terms.

829. Economy is the art of making the most of life.
George Bernard Shaw

830. It is not doing the thing we like to do, but liking to do the things we have to do, that makes life blessed.
Johann Wolfgang Goethe

(See also: Man.)

LOVE

831. In the triangle of love between ourselves, God and other people is found the secret of existence, and the best foretaste, I suspect, that we can have on earth of what heaven will probably be like.
Samuel M. Shoemaker

832. What men commonly call love is usually an affectation which shuns like the plague truth between people. Where there is no will to truth, even sacrifice turns to flattery.
Knud E. Logstrup

833. Love does not parade the imperfections of others or taunt men for their weaknesses. Rather love seeks to understand men—their imperfections and weaknesses.

834. We are shaped and fashioned by what we love.
Johann Wolfgang Goethe

835. To be loved means to be consumed. To love is to give light with inexhaustible oil. To be loved is to pass away; to love is to endure.
Rainer Maria Rilke

836. If thy love be pure, simple, and well ordered, thou shalt be free from the bondage of things.
Thomas a Kempis

837. There are many things love cannot condone, but there is nothing love cannot face.

838. When we love, we give up the center of ourselves.
Rollo May

839. Equality is a quantitative term and, therefore, love knows nothing of it. Authority exercised with humility, and obedience accepted with delight are the very lines along which our spirits live.
C. S. Lewis

840. For where love is wanting, the beauty of all virtue is mere tinsel, is empty sound, is not worth a straw, nay more, is offensive and disgusting.

John Calvin

841. The contemporary search for love is mostly the consequence of a desire for the results of love with no corresponding willingness to share the sacrifice of love.

842. Love is its own reason for being—it needs no other justification.

843. He drew a circle that shut me out—
Heretic, rebel, a thing to flout.
But Love and I had the wits to win:
We drew a circle that took him in.

Edwin Markham

844. Nothing angers a man more than to be discovered in his hatred by love.

845. The decisive test of one's belonging to Christ is not reception of baptism, nor partaking of the Lord's Supper, but solely and exclusively a union with Christ through faith which shows itself active in love.

Emil Brunner

846. One day Sydney Harris of the *Chicago Daily News* walked with his friend to a newsstand to purchase a paper. The friend thanked the vendor politely, but the vendor remained coldly silent. As they moved away, Harris remarked: "A sullen fellow, isn't he?" And the friend replied: "Oh, he's that way every night." Harris asked: "Well, why then do you continue to be so very polite to him?" His friend answered: "Why should I let him decide how I'm going to act?"

847. One loving heart sets another on fire.

Saint Augustine

848. Compassion without morality is sentimental and effusive while morality without compassion is cold and inhumane.

Kenneth Keniston

849. Goodness that grows from the Spirit is not done on the basis of "I'll be good to you if you'll be good to me" but [on the basis of] "God is good to me, and I'll share His goodness with you."

(See also: Compassion; Interpersonal Relations; Love For Enemies; Love For God.)

LOVE FOR ENEMIES

850. In taking revenge a man is but even with his enemy. But in passing it over he is superior.
Francis Bacon

851. The Christian doesn't turn the other cheek because it is a technique calculated to passively overcome one's opponent. The cheek is turned because you are surrendered to Christ and you love Him by loving his creatures.

852. Nothing annoys an enemy so much as having his painful remarks quickly forgotten.
James E. Harrison

853. Love for enemies does not mean to help them accomplish their sinister purposes.
Daniel Poling

854. Loving your enemy does not prohibit you from opposing him, of stopping him, or even defeating him. There is nothing in the Christian concept of love that requires you to support an enemy's desire to destroy you. Submit—yes. But support—never!

855. Jesus didn't say: "Don't have enemies." He said: "Love your enemies." To love an enemy is not to support his prejudice against you either by default or design. It is to do what is in your enemy's best interest.

856. Some years ago an army officer was suddenly overcome with rage and he struck a soldier in the face. The soldier, who was just a private in rank, restrained himself and gave the officer a simple but provocative response. He said: "Sir, I'll make you sorry for that if it's the last thing I ever do!"

Some months later these same two men—the officer and the private—were in battle, fighting against a common enemy. The private suddenly noticed that the officer was in trouble—pinned down by enemy fire and slightly wounded. The private fought his way to the officer's side and together they fought their way back to their own lines. And when they reached a place of safety, the officer—very moved by what the private had done—extended his hand in genuine friendship and said: "What a return for the insult I gave you." The soldier gripped the officer's hand and softly said: "I told you, sir, that I would make you sorry for that if it was the last thing I ever did."

LOVE FOR GOD

857. You only love Jesus as much as the person you love the least.

858. A woman with a torch and jug was asked: "Where are you going?" She replied: "To burn the pleasures of heaven and quench the flames of hell so people will love God for His own sake."

(See also: Commitment; Self-Denial; Surrender.)

LOYALTY

859. If you are ashamed to stand by your colors, you had better seek another flag.

LUCK

860. I never knew an early rising, hardworking, prudent man who complained of hard luck.

Joseph Addison

861. Luck is that point in life where opportunity and preparation meet.

Gary Gariepy

M

MAN

862. Those who deny the existence of God are hard put to explain the existence of man.

Harold Berry

863. The truth about man is that he needs to be loved most when he deserves it the least. Only God can fulfill this incredible need. Only God can provide a love so deep it redeems from the depths.

864. A beast does not know that he is a beast, and the nearer a man gets to being a beast, the less he knows it.

George MacDonald

865. Three monkeys sat in a coconut tree,
Discussing things as they're said to be.
Said one to the others: Now listen you two,
There's a certain rumor that can't be true.
That man has descended from our noble race,
Why, the very idea is an utter disgrace.
No monkey ever deserted his wife,
Starved her baby and ruined her life.
And you've never known a mother monk
To leave her babies with others to bunk,
And passing them on from one to the other,
Till they scarcely knew which one was their mother.
And another thing you'll never see
Is a monk building a fence 'round a coconut tree,
Forbidding all other monks to taste,
And letting the coconuts go to waste.
Why if I'd build a fence 'round my coconut tree,
Starvation would force you to steal from me.
And another thing a monk won't do,
Is to go out at night and get on a stew,
And use a club, a gun, or a knife
To take some other monkey's life.
Yes, man descended, the noble cuss,
But, brother, he didn't descend from us.

866. It is easier to understand human nature if one bears in mind the fact that almost everyone thinks he is an exception to most rules.

867. The great need of the human heart is "to untie things that are now knotted together, and tie up things that are still dangling loose."

C. S. Lewis

868. Man by the Fall fell at the same time from his state of innocency and from his dominion over nature. Both of these losses, however, even in this life, can in some part be repaired; the former by religion and faith, and the latter by the arts and sciences.

Francis Bacon

869. Until a man has found God, he begins at no beginning and ends at no end.

H. G. Wells

870. When God made us in His own image, He gave a mind that we may know, a will that we may decide, and a heart that we may desire and love. What great potential for good, but also what tremendous capacity for evil.

George Gritter

871. Man's conquest of nature has been astonishing. His failure to conquer human nature has been tragic.

Julius Mark

872. God does not love us because we are valuable. We are valuable because God loves us.

Fulton J. Sheen

873. What a chimera then is man. What a novelty! What a monster, what a chaos, what a contradiction, what a prodigy! Judge of all things, imbecile worm of the earth; depository of truth, a sink of uncertainty and error; the pride and refuse of the universe.

Blaise Pascal

874. In the presence of God there is no such thing as status; for in the presence of God every man . . . is nothing more than a hell-deserving sinner.

William Barclay

875. This is a jaded world; man is played out. The world is like a ship at sea with savages climbing on board and taking over the chart room. It is void of recuperative power.

H. G. Wells

876. We are not part of a nice neat creation, set in motion by a loving God; we are part of a mutinous world where rebellion against God is the order of the day.

Samuel M. Shoemaker

877. If a man wants God to leave him alone, that is what will happen—forever.

M. P. Horban

878. The tragedy of modern man is that his emptiness is not a feeling but a reality.

(See also: Life.)

MARRIAGE

879. The sex experience between spouses is only creative and psychologically productive when it is at the same time both self-searching and self-giving. This level of experience is seldom embraced because it only comes at that point when the egos mutually put down their defenses.

880. For a married person, flirting is never innocent.

881. The Christian church says to every bridegroom: "Through this woman you are to explore the whole of womankind. If you turn elsewhere, seeking more, you will in fact find less." And this principle applies equally to the bride.

882. At his fiftieth wedding anniversary Henry Ford was asked: "What is the formula for a good marriage?" He replied: "The same as for a successful car; stick to one model."

883. It is right to be jealous "for" someone else. It is good for husbands and wives to be jealous for each other's love.

G. Aiken Taylor

884. In the ideal marriage husband and wife are not loyal to each other because it is their duty, but because it is their joy.

E. Merrill Root

885. Successful marriage is always a triangle: a man, a woman, and God.

Cecil Myers

886. Every man who is happily married is a successful man, even if he has failed in everything else.

William Lyon Phelps

887. If you cannot receive, your giving will be a domination of the partner. If you cannot give, your receiving will leave you empty.

Rollo May

888. Money is not a main problem in marriage. It is only the battleground. The real problem is that husband and wife cannot negotiate their differences of opinion.

889. Marriage is more than finding the right person. It is being the right person.

890. J. Paul Getty, the richest man in the world, once said of marriage: "I deeply regret the failure of my five marriages. But I recognized long ago that a man who was going to be a big success in business wasn't going to stand much of a chance as a husband."

891. The man who marries the wrong woman either becomes a cynic or a philosopher.

892. Marriage is a gamble. You start with a pair. He shows a diamond. She shows a heart. Her father has a club. His father has a spade. There is usually a joker around somewhere. But after awhile he becomes a king and she becomes a queen. Then they end up with a full house. And that's where the game of life really begins.

893. In a quiz show on the New Testament a small boy was asked: "What did Jesus say about people getting married?" The child answered without hesitation: "Jesus said, 'Forgive them for they know not what they do.' "

894. There's not a good marriage in existence that couldn't be made better.

895. Poor motivation in childhood usually produces a poor marriage.

MATERIALISM AND HEDONISM

896. American men and women spend 18 percent more on cosmetic products and services than on all religious and welfare activities combined. Many Christians spend more for cosmetics than they give to world missions.

897. The difference between Patrick Henry and the average American today is that Patrick Henry said: "Give me liberty or give me death," and the average American today just says: "Gimme."

Vance Havner

898. Happiness is the fulfillment of the total self. The

pleasure seeker is usually an unhappy person because his search and his find are relevant only to a part of himself, while much of his "total self" goes unfilled.

899. Americans often spend more than they make on things they don't need to impress people they don't like.

900. Prosperity is only an instrument to be used; not a deity to be worshiped.
Calvin Coolidge

901. Lustful ambition breeds the fools who bid for counterfeit kingdoms. From such preserve us, Good Lord.
Richard John Neuhaus

902. A man is rich in proportion to the number of things he can afford to let alone.
Henry David Thoreau

903. Success, achievement, social life, family, friends, health, marvelous physiques—all of these lie if they promise to satisfy deep heart hungers. Because only Jesus can.
Keith Wegemann

904. Christian discipleship has got to be more than driving to church once a week in the latest model car while in between time vegetating in front of a thousand-dollar television console.

905. That which is experienced by the physical senses can never satisfy the spirit. Hence, there is much spiritual emptiness in the midst of pleasure and plenty.

906. Poverty won't help you get into heaven, but riches may keep you out.

907. We are continuously brain-washed and pistol-whipped by mass media's repeated assertions that life's only worthy pursuits are money and sex, that life's only excitement is violence, and that life's only fulfillment is success. There is, however, a way of deliverance, but it lies not in the direction so brightly signposted by the media—out of the ego not into it; heads lifted up from the trough instead of buried in it. Then see how worldly wisdom pales in the purifying sunburst of everlasting truth.

908. What we need in life is not a series of events that will make big money, but rather a big event that will make money—even big money—look small.

909. The trouble with "eat, drink, and be merry, for tomorrow we die," is that we usually don't die tomorrow, but instead live on to reap only too fully the negative consequences of shortsighted pleasure seeking.

O. Hobart Mowrer

910. If you want to destroy a nation, give it too much—make it greedy, miserable and sick.

John Steinbeck

911. America has more things than any other nation in the world, and more books on how to find happiness.

W. E. Sangster

912.   Since all the riches of this world
    May be the gifts from the devil and earthly kings,
    I should suspect that I worshipped the devil
    If I thanked my God for worldly things.

William Blake

913. We like to think that all the evil of the world is concentrated in the Kremlin, and I for one believe it an outpost of hell, with demonic power possessing its leaders and their followers. But who of us, and what nations of the world, have not had a hand in making today's world? Half of America is avowedly godless. Much of the Christian church is halfhearted. Our real hearts are in money and power and success.

Samuel M. Shoemaker

914. We need to get out of our gold-plated ruts because a rut is a shallow grave.

915. Money can buy the husk of many things, but not the kernel. It brings you food, but not appetite; medicine, but not health; acquaintances, but not friends; servants, but not faithfulness; days of joy, but not peace and happiness.

Henrik Ibsen

916. Material abundance without character is the surest way to destruction.

Thomas Jefferson

917. The only ultimate disaster that can befall us is to feel ourselves at home on this earth.

Malcolm Muggeridge

918.   Pleasures are like poppies spread;
    You seize the flower and the bloom is shed.

Robert Burns

919. The golden calf is kicking us to death.

920. Not long ago I heard of a sincere man who said: "Last year I only made $30,000, but this year I really obeyed the Lord and made my first half-million." One begins to wonder, why then did Jesus end up without a penny on a cross?

Arthur E. Sueltz

921. Things [material] are in the saddle and ride mankind.

Ralph Waldo Emerson

922. There is a lot of talk about deprived persons today. Many persons seem to feel deprived if anyone has more than they do.

923. Absolutely speaking, the more money the less virtue.

Henry David Thoreau

MATURITY

924. Some people never grow up—they just grow old. Many a woman has a teenage husband and many a longsuffering male has a child bride with wrinkles.

(See also: Character.)

MEEKNESS

925. It's the nature of God to make something out of nothing; therefore, when anyone is nothing, God may yet make something of him.

Martin Luther

MEN

926. Nothing is more dangerous than weak men who think they are tough guys.

I. F. Stone

927. Not how did he die?
But how did he live?
Not what did he gain?
But what did he give?
These are the units
To measure the worth
Of a man as a man
Regardless of birth.

Not what was his station?
But had he a heart?
And how did he play
His God-given part?

Was he always ready
With words of good cheer,
To bring back a smile,
And to banish a tear?

928. God give us men! A time like this demands
Strong minds, great hearts, true faith and ready hands;
Men whom the lust of office does not kill;
Men whom the spoils of office cannot buy;
Men who possess opinions and a will;
Men who have honor, men who will not lie.

Josiah Gilbert Holland

929. American men are, by their own weakness, forcing their women to become men, and for that neither God nor nature will ever forgive them. Nor will women.

Taylor Caldwell

930. Nobody knows what a boy is worth,
And the world must wait and see,
For every man in an honored place,
Is a boy that used to be.

931. That men prefer hard-to-get women misses the point. Men really adore women who are hard for other men to get.

MENTAL HEALTH

932. The Bible has as much to say about resting as about working. Our Lord would have us come apart and rest awhile, for if we don't we will just come apart.

Vance Havner

933. The degree of mental illness a Christian experiences is in proportion to his spiritual maturity.

Lee Fisher

934. A Bible that is falling apart usually belongs to someone who isn't.

935. Despair is a secret destroyer of the human spirit, as real and as deadly a menace to our cultural sanity as the misused power of the atom is to our physical survival.

Theodore Roszak

936. Emotions were made to enjoy—but out of control they tend to destroy.

Lyle Flinner

937. The self-centered are the self-disrupted.

E. Stanley Jones

938. Our feelings of depression and despair tell more about ourselves than about the way things really are.

939. What isolates the patient the most in his life—whether schoolboy, housewife or worker—is the very thing that isolates [all of] us the most: our secrets.

Paul Tournier

940. Reality continuously crushes to death those who close themselves in defensively.

Edward Glynn

941. Express your feelings and you ride them. Repress your feelings and they ride you.

942. The important thing in life is not how you look in other people's eyes, but what you know about yourself.

943. A man once attempted to assassinate Franklin Roosevelt. The man was apprehended and interrogated. One of the questions he was asked was: "Do you belong to a church?" He answered: "No, I belong only to myself and I suffer."

944. Modern man is often one whose daily intake of pep pills balances his daily intake of tranquilizers sufficiently to enable him to make a weekly trip to the psychiatrist.

945. The neurotic doesn't know what it means to be genuine—to feel good about his strengths and to be candid about his weaknesses in a nondefensive way. He is committed to presenting a facade that he thinks people will like and that will help him cope with anxiety.

946. The predominant characteristic of a neurotic person is an excessive dependence on the approval and affection of others, the need for recognition and success.

Karen Horney

(See also: The Mind; Peace of Mind; Self-Pity; Suffering.)

THE MIND

947. Men of intemperate minds cannot be free. Their passions forge their fetters.

Edmund Burke

THE MINISTER

948. A preacher should have the mind of a scholar, the

heart of a child and the hide of a rhinoceros. His biggest problem is how to toughen his hide without hardening his heart.

Vance Havner

949. A ministry that is college-educated and seminary-trained, but not Spirit-filled, works no miracles.

Samuel Chadwick

950. To become ordained is not necessarily to escape from one's passion for power. It may only serve to canonize it.

Ian Henderson

951. Value, in this country, is demonstrated by money, and the poor salary or honorarium paid to the preacher is an indication of the small value in which he is held by people who understand the meaning of money in every other regard.

952. The preacher, it is true, isn't in the ministry for money. But that is no excuse for insisting that he live without it.

953. A pastor's first duty is to equip the saints—not to outshine them.

954. Avoid, as you would the plague, a clergyman who is also a man of business.

Jerome

955. The very moment clerics become worldly, the world goes to hell.

Arthur Hertzberg

956. It is not the business of the preacher to fill the house. It is his business to fill the pulpit.

Vance Havner

957. The effective preacher needs a fresh and finely-focused vision of the holiness of God, the destructiveness of sin and the lostness of man.

958. If you are a minister, God expects you to wear at least two hats. You are a soldier sliding on your belly into enemy territory, cutting the barbed wires of superstition to set the captives of Satan free. And then you are a shepherd, feeding and protecting the ones you helped free.

Dick Hillis

MIRACLES

959. To those who believe God, a miracle needs no

explanation; to those who don't, no explanation will suffice.

(See also: Divine Healing.)

MODESTY

960. When the worldly women decided to appear less modest by hiking up their hemlines, why did church women follow suit? To glorify Christ or to worship at the beloved altar of conformity?

961. [The girl] needs to combine attractiveness and modesty at the same time. If she is attractive without being modest, she directs the desire of the boy to her body. If she's unattractive and only modest, she doesn't have the date in the first place. But if she is modest or careful, she directs the desire of the boy to her soul and he's willing to pay the price for getting that girl.

Walter Trobisch

962. Choice of clothing does not make one a Christian. But one's choice of clothing can keep him from being Christian and Christ-like.

963. Christian modesty and worldly pride are like fire and water. When mixed, one destroys the other.

964. If what my eyes behold on the street and also in the churches is any indication, clothes are no longer made to cover the body, but to decorate it.

965. One of the most obvious forms of erotic self-display is clothes. In our time, despite the herculean efforts of *Esquire* and, later, *Playboy*, only relatively slight progress has been made toward converting men's fashions into effective means for erotic display. Dramatically colored sports garb and the present apparently waning fashion of white shirts are evidence that men are not unaware that color and variety enhance their sexual attractiveness. . . .

Andrew M. Greeley

966. Jesus Christ said that a certain type of gaze constituted adultery in God's eyes. Should we, who claim faith in this Christ, use rapidly changing customs as an excuse to court adultery by a loose manner, or indecent exposure of the body? The Christian woman will never do what tempts a man to mental lust.

MONEY

967. What we need in life is not a series of events that

will make big money, but rather a big event that will make money—even big money—look small.

968. Money is not able to buy one single necessity of the soul.

Henry David Thoreau

969. Money still talks; it usually says "Goodbye."

970. It is difficult to save money when your neighbors keep buying things you can't afford.

971. Dug from the mountain side,
 Washed in the glen,
 Servant am I or master of men.
 Steal me, I curse you;
 Earn me, I bless you;
 Grasp me and hoard me,
 A fiend shall possess you.
 Live for me, die for me,
 Covet me, take me,
 Angel or devil,
 I am what you make me.

972. The lack of money is the root of all organizational cooperation.

973. Money is like manure. Stack it up and it stinks; spread it around and it makes things grow.

MORALITY

(See: Character; Immorality; Integrity; Truth: United States—Moral Climate.)

MOTHERHOOD

974. An eight-year-old boy gave the following description of mothers. "They make you wash your ears every day and they can tell if you don't brush your teeth—even if you wet the toothbrush."

975. The most important occupation on earth for a woman is to be a real mother to her children. It does not have much glory to it; there is a lot of grit and grime. But there is no greater place of ministry, position or power than that of a mother.

Phil Whisenhunt

(See also: Parenthood.)

MOTIVES

976. The last temptation is the greatest treason:
 To do the right deed for the wrong reason.

T. S. Eliot

MOVIES

977. Hollywood is a place where ten million dollars worth of machinery functions to put skin on baloney.
George Jean Nathan

MUSIC

978. Music is, in her health, the teacher of perfect order, and is the voice of obedience of angels, and the companion of the courses of the spheres of heaven; but in her depravity she is also the teacher of perfect disorder and disobedience.

John Ruskin

979. The use of bad music for a good goal does not alter the music's character, only the character of those who use it.

980. The contemporary obsession to grasp the glamor of innovative techniques serves only to mask our own emptiness.

N

THE NATION

981. If you are not willing to take care of your nation-state, the state will soon be taking care of you.

982. A church will destroy itself by professing a truth it does not obey. Likewise a society will destroy itself by failing to demand strict adherence to its laws.

983. Almighty God, who has given us this good land for our heritage, we humbly beseech Thee that we may always prove ourselves a people mindful of Thy favor and glad to do Thy will. Bless our land with honorable industry, sound learning, and pure manners. Save us from violence, discord, and confusion; from pride and arrogancy, and from every evil way. Defend our liberties and fashion into one united people the multitudes brought out of many kindreds and tongues. Endure with the spirit of wisdom those whom in Thy name we entrust the authority of government, that there may be peace and justice at home, and that through obedience to Thy law, we may show forth Thy praise among the nations of the earth. In the time of prosperity, fill our hearts with thankfulness, and in the day of trouble, suffer not our trust in Thee to fail. All of which we ask through Jesus Christ, our Lord, Amen.

George Washington

984. What this country needs is a man who knows God other than by hearsay.

Thomas Carlyle

(See also: Patriotism.)

NEUTRALITY

985. The world is rushing to Armageddon where no one sits on the fence.

Charles R. Hembree

986. The hottest places in hell are reserved for those who, in a period of moral crisis, maintain their neutrality.

Dante

NEW BIRTH

987. You can't explain the mystery of the physical birth—so don't feel compelled to explain the mystery of the "new birth." Just make sure that you have, by God's grace, been born again.

Sam Hart

988. It always seemed absurd to me
To sing of "such a worm as I,"
Until I saw an ugly worm
Become a gorgeous butterfly.

(See also: Conversion; Salvation.)

THE NEW YEAR

989. FOR NEW YEAR'S DAY

O take the new year by the hand
And face the bright untraveled land
With heart aflame and fearlessly.
It is a wondrous thing to be
At shining thresholds, and to wear
A shield of faith, a cloak of prayer!
Rejoice! On roads sun-swept and new;
Our God has glorious things for you!

Grace V. Watkins

990. People laugh at New Year's resolutions. But we can all use ten minutes in a chair followed by a humble prayer.

991. If you do not think about the future, you cannot have one.

John Galsworthy

992. Begin again—you can, you know.
Seek out a better way to go.
Forget the past—the past is dead,
And all tomorrow lies ahead!
There's never a time too late to start,
To bring to fruition that dream in your heart.
Begin again now, this minute, this day!
A new life is waiting—don't wish it away.

Helen Lowrie Marshall

993. Good resolutions are like babies crying in church. They should be carried out immediately.
Charles M. Sheldon

994. No time for God?
      What fools we are ...
      No time for God?
      As soon to say no time
      To eat, to sleep, to live, to die.
      Take time for God,
      Or a poor misshapen thing you'll be
      To step into eternity,
      And say,
      "I had no time for Thee."

(See also: The Future; Time.)

O

OBEDIENCE

995. Grand programs of action, brilliantly conceived strategems, tight-knit organization, accommodation to contemporary idioms, and institutional astuteness are not adequate substitutes for obedience to Christ.

996. All heaven is waiting to help those who will discover the will of God and do it.

J. Robert Ashcroft

997. One act of obedience is better than one hundred sermons.

Dietrich Bonhoeffer

OLD AGE

998. How do I know
 My youth is all spent?
 Well, my get up and go
 Has got up and went.
 But in spite of it all
 I'm able to grin,
 When I think of the places
 My get up has been.

Lillie Buffum

999. It is magnificent to grow old if one keeps young while doing it.

Harry Emerson Fosdick

1000. You tell me I am getting old,
 I tell you that's not so!
 The house I live in is worn out,
 And that, of course, I know.
 It's been in use a long, long while;
 It's weathered many a gale.
 I'm really not surprised you think
 It's getting somewhat frail.

The color changing on the roof,
The windows getting dim;
The walls a bit transparent,
And looking rather thin.
The foundation not so steady
As once it used to be;
My house is getting shaky,
But my "house" isn't me!

My few short years can't make me old,
I feel I'm in my youth.
Eternity lies just ahead,
A life of joy and truth.
I'm going to live forever, there;
Life will go on—it's grand.
You tell me I am getting old?
You just don't understand!

The dweller in my little "house"
Is young and bright and gay;
Just starting on a life to last
Throughout eternal day.
You see only the outside which
Is all that most folks see;
You tell me I am getting old?
You've mixed my house with me!

OPTIMISM

1001. A possibility is a hint from God.

Soren Kierkegaard

1002. If you will give me a fulcrum which is strong enough and a lever which is long enough, I can move the world.

Archimedes

1003. The optimist proclaims that we live in the best of all possibile worlds; and the pessimist fears this is true.

James B. Cabell

1004. The pessimist sees the difficulty in every opportunity; the optimist sees the opportunity in every difficulty.

Lawrence P. Jacks

ORGANIZATION

1005. We tend to meet any new situation by reorganizing, and a wonderful method it can be for creating an illusion of progress, while producing confusion, inefficiency, and demoralization.

Petronius Arbiter

P

PARENTHOOD

1006. Considering the number of divorces today, it seems that more parents are running away from home than children.

1007. A presupposition of Christianity is that a Christian is in possession of the truth. That being so, it necessarily follows that Christian parents and teachers are committed not only to the instruction of children, but to indoctrination as well—since the ultimate battle in life is truth against non-truth.

1008. The child you want to raise as an upright and honorable person requires a lot more of your time than your money.

George Varky

1009. What greater joy can a parent have than to mold a future saint?

1010. When children obey, the parent should symbolize his love with indulgence. When children disobey, he should symbolize his love with discipline. In both cases and especially in the case of discipline, the parent's love guards the child's best interest while rejecting his own selfish interest by ignoring his popularity-comfort index.

1011. Your children will either hate you till they're twenty-one and love you for the rest of their lives or they'll love you till they're twenty-one and hate you the rest of their lives.

Betty G. Ulrich

1012. If you spent no more than an hour a day on the spiritual development of your children, in eighteen years your total investment of time would be over seven thousand hours. Can a Christian parent afford less?

1013. A permissive home is a home where you don't love enough to exercise the authority that Christ gave you. Quit saying you're broadminded and tolerant. You just lack guts!
Ben Haden

1014. Permissiveness is not a policy; it is the abandonment of policy. And its apparent advantages are illusory.
B. F. Skinner

1015. The point at which most parents lose their children is when the parent needs to speak with authority. The authority which parents have, but often choose to ignore, is the authority given them by God. It comes to the parent by way of a personal knowledge of and a personal surrender to the Word of God. Lacking this authority, and the children being beyond spanking age, there is then no apparent reason for obedience. And to compound what is already a deplorable situation, the parent so desperately desires some semblance of unity in the home that he not only capitulates to but also cooperates with the child's unreasonable, irrational, and nonsensical demands.

1016. If you don't firmly program your children's minds with truth, someone else will do so with half-truth, untruth, and unimportant truth.

1017. Parents don't plan to fail in raising their children—they often fail to plan.

1018. If we work upon marble, it will perish. If we work upon brass, time will efface it. If we rear temples, they will crumble to dust. But if we work upon men's immortal minds, if we imbue them with high principles, with the just fear of God and love of their fellow men, we engrave on those tablets something which no time can efface and which will brighten to all eternity.
Daniel Webster

1019. A best-interest motive plus a best-interest action equals a best-interest love. We parents must do what is best for our children even if it causes us discomfort in the form of hostile reaction.

1020. In our thirty-two years of [medical] practice we have found that the deprivation of normal parental love is involved in almost every nervous breakdown.
Frank S. Caprio; Frances S. Leighton

1021. The frightening fact about heredity and environment is that parents provide both.

1022. Although communication between parents and teens is often nonexistent, teens are really saying: "Be angry with me, care about me, about what I do, about what happens to me." But unless a parent has been angry with his child in the sense of "caring" from infancy, he will find giving such concern a difficult road, and the teen will find this concern difficult to accept, even though he wants it.

1023. The trouble with parenthood is that by the time you're experienced, you're unemployable.

1024. It takes great courage and foresight to say as my father did: "I don't care what you think of me now; I'm concerned with what you will think of me twenty years from now.

Sam Levenson

1025. Parents are so anxious to fulfill their children's needs, to cultivate their abilities, to develop their potential, and to have them so continuously and uninhibitedly happy that they often fail to teach them to honor, consider, and respect the rights of parents.

1026. If a child lives with criticism, he learns to condemn.
   If a child lives with hostility, he learns to fight.
   If a child lives with ridicule, he learns to be shy.
   If a child lives with shame, he learns to feel guilty.
   If a child lives with tolerance, he learns to be patient.
   If a child lives with encouragement, he learns confidence.
   If a child lives with praise, he learns to appreciate.
   If a child lives with fairness, he learns justice.
   If a child lives with security, he learns to have faith.
   If a child lives with approval, he learns to like himself.
   If a child lives with acceptance and friendship, he learns to find love in the world.

Dorothy Law Nolte

1027. I've made this observation
   While browsing 'round the town:
   Some people bring their children up,
   Some people let them down.

F. G. Kernan

1028. An important sign of emotional maturity in the parent is the ability to say yes and to say no at the right times, and to make it stick.

1029. Children quickly comprehend when parents exercise selfish instead of responsible discipline. This insight was put most succinctly by the boy who asked his mother, "Why must I always take a nap when you're tired?"

1030. A missionary father once said: "If I led a thousand heathen to Christ while my own children, through my neglect, went to hell, I'd be a failure as a missionary."

1031. Some argue that in parenthood good psychology will do. I have observed, however, that the child is usually better at psychology than the parent.

S. Hugh Paine

1032. When preaching on how to raise children, Jack Hyles said: "You spoil them, you let them wear long hair and short dresses, you let them listen to ungodly rock music and will never discipline your children . . . you don't love them and when you get old they won't love you. They'll put you in an old folks home and let you rot."

1033. A judge who has been involved in a great many family cases said: "We adults spend far too much time preparing the path for our youth and far too little time preparing our youth for the path."

1034. If we had paid no more attention to our plants than we have to our children, we would now be living in a jungle of weeds.

Luther Burbank

PASSION

1035. Nazism would never have established so firm a grip if, from the outset, it had been faced by Christians as enthusiastic for what is true as the Nazis were for what is false.

Edward Halifax

1036. Most great men and women are not perfectly rounded in their personalities, but are instead people whose one driving enthusiasm is so great it makes their faults seem insignificant.

Charles A. Cerami

THE PAST

1037. Those who cannot remember the past are condemned to repeat it.

George Santayana

(See also: History; Time.)

PATRIOTISM

1038. If you are ashamed to stand by your colors, you had better seek another flag.

1039. Communism flourishes only where patriotism does not.

J. Kesner Kahn

1040. The man or woman who reserves the right to do nothing, who will not participate in a collective action of the United States, shouldn't be around for the dividends.

Lewis B. Hershey

1041. Patriotism is the praiseworthy competition with one's ancestors.

Tacitus

1042. True patriotism is not manifested in short frenzied bursts of emotion. It is the tranquil steady dedication of a lifetime.

Adlai E. Stevenson

1043. Nothing will ruin the country if the people themselves will undertake its safety; and nothing can save it if they leave their safety in any hands but their own.

Daniel Webster

1044. Breathes there a man with soul so dead,
   Who never to himself hath said,
   This is my own, my native land!

Sir Walter Scott

(See also: The Nation.)

PEACE

1045. The only men who do not serve in some army are those who are ruled by someone else's army. Without power you must do as you are told. When you lay down your arms, it's not the saints who will come marching in.

1046. I am a pacifist but if we can't have peace without fighting for it, then let us fight with all our hearts.

Henry Ford

1047. If "peace" means an all-Communist world of captive nations under Soviet rule, then the U.N. is indeed the best hope for "peace."

J. Kesner Kahn

1048. To be prepared for war is one of the most effectual means of preserving peace.

George Washington

1049. The peace is won by accompanying God into the battle.

Eivind Josef Berggrav

1050. Peace is not the absence of conflict but the presence of God no matter what the conflict.

1051. Real integrity will survive the worst of blood baths, but no peace, however placid, will suffice to preserve a decaying and spiritually depraved world.

1052. PEACE also stands for *P*eople *E*xisting *A*fter *C*ommunist *E*nslavement.

J. Kesner Kahn

(See also: Peace of Mind.)

PEACE OF MIND

1053. For the Christian who has learned with Saint Paul "in whatsoever state I am therein to be content," there is nothing in this world that a bended knee at the throne of grace will not take care of.

1054. When at night you cannot sleep, talk to the Shepherd and stop counting sheep.

1055. Thou has created us after Thyself, O God, and our hearts are restless till they rest in Thee.

Saint Augustine

1056. The native element of the bird is air, and that of the fish is water. Spiritually speaking, the native element of man is the Kingdom of God. So, for the most part, man is outside his element; and outside of that Kingdom, man can never be at peace with himself.

(See also: Contentment; Fulfillment.)

PENITENCE

1057. While God treats us [Christians] as if we had never sinned, we must never treat God as if we had never sinned.

Oscar F. Reed

1058. I have carried a penitent form around in my heart for half a century or more, and if there is ever any need, instantly I fly there. Jesus waits, loves, pities, and never turns away the seeking soul.

Samuel Brengle

PENTECOST

1059. Men ablaze are invincible. For fifty days the facts of the Gospel were complete, but no conversions were recorded. Pentecost registered three thousand the first day.

Samuel Chadwick

1060. Pentecost was its own publicity.

Vance Havner

PERMISSIVENESS

1061. Permissiveness is not a policy; it is the abandonment of policy. And its apparent advantages are illusory.

B. F. Skinner

PERSECUTION

1062. If someone's sense of security depends on having all men speak well of him, he can never be secure in following Christ.

Calvin Miller

1063. If through faith in Christ you can claim with Saint Paul victory over the awful specter of death, you stand invincible against both puns and persecution.

1064. A Christian is someone who shares the sufferings of God in the world.

Dietrich Bonhoeffer

1065. Bearing wrong is a glorious part of the fellowship with Christ's sufferings; a glorious mark of being conformed to His most holy likeness; a most blessed fruit of the true life of faith.

Andrew Murray

1066. Truth is hard and uncompromising at times. Its followers are a hardy breed and more often than not they are despised and rejected.

1067. Some time ago a group of Christians in Red China got a message through to friends in Hong Kong: "Has the rapture taken place and are we left behind?"

PERSEVERANCE

1068. When you come to the end of your rope—tie a knot and hold on.

1069. ### ANSWER

Full half a hundred times I've sobbed,
  I can't go on! I can't go on!
And yet full half a hundred times
  I've hushed my sobs, and gone.

My answer, if you ask me how,
  May seem presumptuously odd,
But I think that what kept keeping on
  When I could not, was God.

Jane Merchant

PERSONAL EVANGELISM

1070. What if you were offered one thousand dollars for every person you led to Christ—would you work harder at it then?

1071. Evangelism is one starving beggar telling another where to find food.

Daniel T. Niles

1072. We evangelicals will fight the liberals when they say there is no hell, but we ... don't take the risk of opening our homes to those going there in an effort to rescue them.

Francis A. Schaeffer

(See also: Christian Witness.)

PERSPECTIVE

1073. Don't trust your eyes when your imagination is out of focus.

Mark Twain

1074. A wholly this-worldly perspective lacks the resonance of a divine concern in its inward vitality.

William Ernest Hocking

PERSUASION

1075. Hitler swayed people with three rules: make it simple, say it often, and make it burn.

H. V. Kaltenborn

PESSIMISM

1076. A pessimist is one who blows out the light to see how dark it is.

Bishop Woodcock

1077. The optimist proclaims that we live in the best of all possible worlds; and the pessimist fears this is true.

James B. Cabell

1078. Some people are making such thorough preparation for rainy days that they aren't enjoying today's sunshine.

William Feather

1079. The pessimist is a person who is seasick during the entire voyage of life.

F. G. Kernan

1080. The pessimist sees the difficulty in every opportunity; the optimist sees the opportunity in every difficulty.

Lawrence P. Jacks

PHARISAISM

1081. We are God's elect!
       Let all the rest be damned!
       There's room in hell for them.
       We don't want heaven crammed!

1082. Holier-than-thou-ism wears many hats and they all cover the eyes.

Handel H. Brown

1083. When self-deception combines with self-seeking, the result is self-righteousness.

1084. The greatest sin is to be conscious of none.

PHILOSOPHY

1085. If philosophers could always agree on the meaning of words, practically all their controversies would vanish.

René Descartes

PIETY

1086. While the Christian should not be vainly proud of his humility or of his symbolic acts which reflect meekness and purity, he should delight in the fact that he is free, through Christ, from conformity. To delight in such freedom is not a pride of piety, though it may be described as such by those who wish to justify their own preoccupation with the presumed comforts of conformity.

PLANNING

1087. Before everything else, getting ready is the secret of success.

Henry Ford

1088. Battles are really won in the preparation effort made for them.

W. T. Purkiser

1089. The shortest distance from where you are to the place where you would like to be is a plan.

PLEASURE

(See: Materialism and Hedonism.)

POISE

1090. Poise is the ability to be at ease conspicuously.

POLITICS AND GOVERNMENT

1091. In our time, political speech and writing are largely a defense of the indefensible.

George Orwell

1092. An absolutism [a kingdom] can do without a faith; a democracy cannot.

Alexis de Tocqueville

1093. In some societies losers do not matter very much. They can be sent to rest homes and asylums, dispatched to distant wars, or thrown in jail. But the success of a peaceful democratic society is dependent on what happens to the people who lose.

1094. The reason so many congressmen are anxious to be reelected is that they would hate to try to make a living under the laws they passed.

1095. The role of government is to develop the strengths, and not play upon the weaknesses, of the individual citizen.

James M. Wall

1096. Of the 3.5 billion people in the world, all but 36 million have received [foreign] aid from the United States.

Congressman Otto Passman

1097. Today in the cry, "Why doesn't the government do something?" we have the twentieth century equivalent of the demand made upon Samuel. It is not merely a cry of desperation; it is an admission of personal moral failure.

G. Aiken Taylor

1098. A Communist shoots our President with a rifle. Conservatives' solution: outlaw Communists. Liberals' solution: outlaw rifles.

E. J. Canavan

1099. If the problem is narcotics, we Americans look to the government to correct the problem. If the problem is alcoholism, we look to the government for an answer. If it is taking care of the aged, we look to the government to fulfill this need. After a recent earthquake in California, one family even sued the government because their home was destroyed.... Government cannot take care of spiritual and moral problems.

Jack E. Noble

1100. Politicians are often the kind of men who would cut down a tree and then stand on the stump and give a speech about conservation.

1101. How badly a congressman's political fence needs mending depends on how much he has straddled it.

1102. Moderate: a fellow who makes enemies left and right.

1103. Politician: "We'll conquer poverty even if it bankrupts us."

1104. What humanity needs is someone who can save it from people who are out to save humanity.

1105. Government is not reason; it is not eloquence; it is force! Like fire, it is a dangerous servant and a fearful master.

George Washington

1106. So meaningless has the electoral process become that the most persistent activity of the candidates is not to discuss issues but to gain "name recognition."

Sidney Lens

1107. The great question of our time is not communism versus individualism, not Europe versus America nor East versus West. It is whether man can bear to live without God.

Will Durant

1108. Pilgrims came to America to establish a social order in which the governing principle would be that a man with the Bible in his hand doesn't need a king to tell him what to do.

G. Aiken Taylor

1109. Theology teaches us what ends are desirable and what means are lawful, while politics teaches what means are effective.

C. S. Lewis

1110. Who wants power wants trouble. Who has power has trouble.

Milton Mayer

1111. Men can be trusted with their own and other men's destinies and be truly free men only so long as they live in obedience to a higher authority—the authority of God.

Thomas Jefferson

1112. Democracy is the worst form of government under the sun—except for all the rest.

Winston Churchill

1113. A disposition to preserve and an ability to improve, taken together, would be my standard of a statesman.

Edmund Burke

1114. The hardest thing about any political campaign is how to win without proving that you are unworthy of winning.

Adlai E. Stevenson

1115. It is one of the political facts of life that power without the effective will to use it is ultimately no power at all. This is the clear and unmistakable message from Cuba, Korea, and Vietnam.

1116. Jesus began one of His parables by saying unto His disciples: "There was in a city a judge, which feared not God, neither regarded man." Presumably, the Master knew His audience would be familiar with this type of judge. So are we!

Medford Evans

POPULARITY

1117. The number of people who believe a thing to be true does not even create a presumption about it one way or the other.

William G. Sumner

PORNOGRAPHY

1118. The city council of Santa Cruz, California, decided to take no action on a proposed ordinance outlawing nude dancing. Councilwoman Anne Garni declared that the proposed law's listing of which portions of the female anatomy are not fit for public view was so obscene that she couldn't even ask a secretary to type it.

1119. If our courts can define God and get prayer out of the public schools, how come they can't define obscenity and get pornography off public shelves?

1120. Most of the dirty books are produced by idiots for idiots.

David Wilkerson

POWER

1121. If we are to possess power, we must surrender all desire to use it for our own ends.

1122. The power of your right arm is only a shadow compared with the inward power of your will, imagination, and desire.

William Law

1123. Power can ennoble as well as corrupt; it can liberate as well as enslave. Self-righteousness is not the exclusive vice of the strong. There is the arrogance of the weak who equate their weakness with virtue and the power of others with vice. There is the self-righteousness of the noninvolved who equate their aloofness with purity and the agonizing involvement of others with evil.

Ernest W. Lefever

1124. There is a fine line between desire to have power for accomplishment and desire to have power for domination.

1125. Our degree of "resurrection power" is in direct ratio to our involvement in being crucified with Christ.

1126. Do you want the power of God? It's something to ponder because divine power will enable you to suffer—creatively.

PRAISE

1127. Our praise for mercy granted should be as earnest as our prayer for mercy needed.

1128. The Christian should be an alleluia from head to foot.

Saint Augustine

1129. Satan is a chronic grumbler. The Christian ought to be a living doxology.

Martin Luther

(See also: Thanksgiving.)

PRAYER

1130. Before we can pray, "Lord, Thy Kingdom come," we must be willing to pray, "My kingdom go."

Alan Redpath

1131. Man is never so tall as when he kneels before God—never so great as when he humbles himself before God. And the man who kneels to God can stand up to anything.

Louis H. Evans

1132. Time will convince even the blindest and most frivolous of us that happiness is no more to be found in the places we usually look than it is to be dug out of the earth. But the man who knows the secret of prayer lives at the top of human happiness.

William Law

1133. Who rises from prayer a better man, his prayer is answered.

George Meredith

1134. Prayer is the nearest approach to God and the highest enjoyment of Him that we are capable of in this life.

William Law

1135. Prayer never excuses sloth. And neither does prayer excuse a lack of initiative. Prayer that does not lead one to action is little more than blasphemy. This point is effectively made in a prayer by Sir Thomas More: "Those things, good Lord, that we pray for, give us also the grace to labor for."

1136. The great tragedy of life is not unanswered prayer, but unoffered prayer.

Frederick B. Meyer

1137. The chief purpose of prayer is that God may be glorified in the answer.

Reuben A. Torrey

1138. More things are wrought by prayer than this world dreams of. Wherefore, let thy voice rise like a fountain . . . night and day.

Alfred Lord Tennyson

1139. God answers prayer immediately. Wish fulfillment is something else.

1140. The first meeting of the early church, after Jesus ascended into heaven, was a prayer meeting.

1141. He who wants anything from God must approach Him with empty hands.

Robert C. Cunningham

1142. To work without praying and without listening [to God] means only to grow and spread oneself upward without striking roots and without an equivalent in the earth.

Helmut Thielicke

1143. Prayer is the most cleansing therapy of the heart and the soul. It converts the "halitosis of hateful speech" into the clean, kind, pure breath of the Spirit.

Carl W. Franke

1144. Satan dreads nothing but prayer. The Devil fears nothing from prayerless studies, prayerless work, prayerless religion. He laughs at our toil, mocks at our wisdom, but he trembles when we pray.

Samuel Chadwick

1145. At the profoundest depths in life, men talk not about God, but with Him.

D. Elton Trueblood

1146. Great supplicants have sought the secret place of the Most High, not that they might escape the world, but that they might learn to conquer it.

Samuel Chadwick

1147. O God, my earth-desires are full of snares;
Forgive and do not answer all my prayers.

1148. A holy life does not always live in the closet, but it cannot live without the closet.

Lincicome

1149. Prayer is listing, listening, learning and living in obedience.

J. Robert Ashcroft

1150. To pray "in Jesus' name" means to pray in His Spirit, in His compassion, in His love, in His outrage, in His concern. In other words, it means to pray a prayer that Jesus himself might pray.

Kenneth L. Wilson

1151. It is not what we ask of God that determines the answer to our prayer, but the motive that prompts the asking. And one might add that most of us find it extremely easy to misread our motives.

1152. The beginning of the power of prayer is not:

"Lord, give something to me." It is rather, "Lord, give me to something."

Kenneth L. Wilson

1153. I know not by what methods rare,
But this I know, God answers prayer.
I know that He has given His Word,
Which tells me prayer is always heard.
And will be answered soon or late,
And so I pray and calmly wait.
I know not if the blessing sought
Will come in just the way I thought.
But leave my prayers with Him alone,
Whose will is wiser than my own,
Assured that He will grant my quest,
Or send some answer far more blest.

1154. True prayer always receives what it asks for—or something better.

Byron Edwards

1155. One psychiatrist has reported that, though he himself does not pretend to be a religious man, he cannot help being impressed by the fact that, in twenty-five years of active practice in New York City, he has never had a patient who really knew how to pray.

William Barclay

1156. No truly advanced soul prays just because of the consequences of praying. The more mature we become, the more we pray just to have fellowship with God and for God to use the fellowship how He will.

W. E. Sangster

1157. If it were the case that whatever we ask, God was pledged to give, then I for one would never pray again, because I would not have sufficient confidence in my own wisdom to ask God for anything.

J. Alec Motyer

PREACHING

1158. The preaching of the Gospel should not be merely for presenting Christ in terms of man's felt wants. (Are you happy? Are you satisfied? Do you want peace of mind? Do you feel that you have failed? Are you fed up with yourself? Do you want a friend? Then come to Christ—as if the Lord Jesus Christ were to be thought of as a fairy godmother or a super psychiatrist.) How can we continue to dish out this kind of chalky lukewarm cereal and yet call it the bread of life? Preaching the Gospel does not mean making capital out of people's anxieties and felt frailties. That is the brainwasher's trick and that is the stock in trade of television commercials. But the preaching of the Gospel should challenge if not compel people to measure their lives by the laws of God.

James I. Packer

1159. No preacher can, at one and the same time, give the impression that he is clever and that God is mighty to save.

James Denney

1160. The best cure for sleeping sickness in the pew is some soul-stirring preaching from the pulpit.

William McPhail

1161. Jesus did not laugh over Jerusalem, He wept over it. When a preacher begins to enjoy his role as prophet, he has begun to fail.

1162. Unstudied thoughts coming from the mind without previous research ... must be of a very inferior quality, even from the most superior men.

Charles Spurgeon

1163. Speaking the truth is important; speaking the truth in love is all-important. Truth without love can become a bludgeon to beat the heart out of a church.

W. T. Purkiser

1164. It is a lazy layman who expects the pastor to come to him and take his spiritual pulse every six months. But it is a most apathetic pastor who has no nourishing food to offer when all his laymen come at once—Sunday morning.

1165. I wouldn't pay a nickel to a preacher who did not preach on hell enough to keep my children afraid of going there.

Seth Rees

1166. The late distinguished Dean of St. Paul's Cathedral in London, William R. Inge, once noted that complaints were being made concerning empty churches. The dean remarked: "I can think of some churches which would be even emptier if the Gospel were preached in them."

1167. Good preaching is terribly expensive in terms of labor and time, but supremely rewarding and profoundly appreciated.

1168. Sometimes a preacher goes all out to skin an old goat, and all he comes up with is a bunch of bleeding lambs.

H. Orton Riley

1169. A prepared messenger is more important than a prepared message.

Robert Munger

1170. When the Holy Spirit fills your mouth, you'll open it. But merely opening your mouth does not assure that the Spirit will fill it.

1171. True eloquence consists in saying all that is necessary and nothing but what is necessary.

Francois de la Rochefoucauld

1172. It is commonplace to say that we have gone through a generation in which the minister has allowed himself to become at best a "pastoral director," and consequently preaching has degenerated. Then, having produced this kind of preaching, which, in all honesty, is not worth listening to, which, as Luther said, would not entice a dog from behind a warm stove, which indeed, people will not sit through, and having fished with this "melancholy bait," we say that preaching is no longer effective. Of course, it isn't effective; how could it be?

Helmut Thielicke

1173. Much of current evangelical preaching is story time and strings of illustrations, rather than sound exposition of the Word of God.

Donald L. Roberts

1174. The charge to Peter was feed my sheep; not try experiments on my rats or even teach my performing dogs new tricks.

C. S. Lewis

1175. A preacher once asked an actor: "Why is it that you can act out a part and move an audience to tears, while I preach Bible truth and people remain unmoved?" Said the actor: "The answer is really quite simple. It is because I act out fiction as if it were truth and you preach truth as if it were fiction."

PREJUDICE

1176. Prejudice is being down on what we're not up on.

THE PRESENT

1177. Trust no future, howe'er pleasant!
Let the dead past bury its dead!
Act,—act in the living present!
Henry Wadsworth Longfellow

1178. This time, like all times, is a very good one, if we but know what to do with it.
Ralph Waldo Emerson

1179. What you do right now has eternity in it.

PRIDE

1180. Whenever we find that our religious life is making us feel that we are good—above all, that we are better than someone else—I think we may be sure that we are being acted on, not by God, but by the Devil. The real test of being in the presence of God is that you either forget about yourself altogether or see yourself as a small dirty object. It is better to forget about yourself altogether.
C. S. Lewis

1181. Some people who never touch intoxicating liquor are, nevertheless, dead drunk with pride, and the wild use of their lips reveals the totality of their self-intoxication.
Haydon L. Gilmore

1182. Criticism is often a form of self-boasting.

1183. No man can really at one and the same time call attention to himself and glorify Christ.
Louis Benes

1184. Some people grow under responsibility; others swell.

1185. Arrogant giving can turn the best of gifts to ashes.
Kenneth L. Wilson

1186. Talk to a man about himself and he will listen for hours.
Benjamin Disraeli

1187. From the headwaters of prideful self-centeredness there flows all manner of wickedness, polluting the countryside with the refuse of sour humanity in union with hell.
James Coulter

1188. The "inner ring," according to C. S. Lewis, is the

group that believes it is exclusive. It is, in Lewis' judgment, not necessarily evil, but he writes: "The desire that draws us into inner rings is another matter. Of all passions, the passion for the inner ring is most skillful in making a man, who is not yet a very bad man, do very bad things."

1189. The scorn of the haughty can claim more casualties than the sword of persecution.

1190. It is a lot easier to work on the world than on ourselves. Arrogance knows this well.

1191. The unforgiving spirit as a pride form is the number one killer of spiritual life.

James Coulter

PRIORITY

1192. Spiritual life is not to be found in merely preferring God over sin, but in preferring God over even a good thing. As Vance Havner points out, the good is often the enemy of the best.

1193. David K. Wachtel said: "Men who wrap themselves in question marks cannot crusade." There is always the danger in every generation that the church will turn to secondary matters.

1194. The people of Treves, Germany, the hometown of Karl Marx, boasted of having more religious buildings than any other town the same size in Europe. The fact was, however, that the town, along with the rest of Europe, was spiritually dead.

1195. You can't get second things by putting them first; you can only get second things by putting first things first.

C. S. Lewis

1196. In the Christian perspective there are just two categories for priorities in life: first and last. Only one concern can occupy the former; everything else falls into the latter.

PROCRASTINATION

1197. God has promised forgiveness to your repentance, but He has not promised tomorrow to your procrastination.

Saint Augustine

PROSPERITY

1198. For every one hundred men who can stand adversity there is only one who can withstand prosperity.
Thomas Carlyle

1199. Prosperity is good campaigning weather for the Devil.

C. S. Lewis

PSYCHIATRY

1200. What psychiatry has done is to bring scientific terminology to the truths that the Bible presents in poetry, allegory and parable.

Smiley Blanton

PURITY

1201. As a psychologist ... let me assure you that there is certainly a case for personal purity.... Personal impurity soils the present, casts a shadow on the future, and brings remorse as you think about the past.
Clyde M. Narramore

PURPOSE

1202. Those who have a "why" to live, can bear with almost any "how."

Victor E. Frankl

1203. The man without purpose is like a ship without a rudder.

Thomas Carlyle

1204. Everything has two handles—one of gold and one of lead. And everything depends on which handle you use to pick it up.

Epictetus

1205. There is no defeat save our own inherent weakness of purpose.

Ralph Waldo Emerson

R

READING

1206. The man who does not read good books has no advantage over the man who cannot read at all.

Mark Twain

REASON

1207. If you are sincere in your search for the Real, you must not repudiate the Rational.

Carl F. H. Henry

REBELLION

1208. Mocking God is life's great impossibility. God is not mocked. The mockery comes back on top of the man who makes it, like the harvest of forgotten seed.

W. T. Purkiser

RECONCILIATION

1209. To reconcile man with man and not with God is to reconcile no one at all.

Thomas Merton

(See also: Interpersonal Relations.)

RECREATION

1210. The Puritans, so often put down by almost everyone, did take time off to play and without benefit of gate receipts.

REFORMATION

1211. Reformation which springs from any source other than regeneration washes only the outside of the cup.

L. Nelson Bell

1212. True reformation is an on-going thing. It is no task, however, for chameleons. The chameleon, says the fable, changes his color to match his surroundings. The reformer changes his surroundings to match his color.

RELIGION

1213. Religion is nothing if it is not the foundation of our whole life.

Robert Thornton

1214. Religious experience is absolute. It is indisputable. You can only say that you have never had such an experience and your opponent will say, "Sorry, I have!"

Carl G. Jung

1215. How a man can receive a particular impression of religion at a certain date and time is to me an inexplicable form of shallowness: to be full of Christmas joy at Christmas time and not to think of Good Friday, to be profoundly sorrowful on Good Friday and not to think of anything else. That is the best proof that religion is something entirely external to one.

Soren Kierkegaard

1216. Religion is meant to be bread for daily use, not cake for special occasions.

1217. What I believe about God is the most important thing about me.

A. W. Tozer

1218. A religious man is one whose life is directed toward something he considers more significant than everything else.

1219. If your religion hasn't changed you, you had better change your religion.

1220. To ascribe to the symbol the efficacy of that which it symbolizes is symbolatry, just as ascribing deity to an idol is idolatry.

1221. Religion is what the individual does with his own solitariness.

Alfred North Whitehead

RENEWAL

1222. The problem for most of us is not how to sustain renewal, but how to get one started.

1223. Society cannot be renewed by people with unrenewed minds, living unrenewed lives. Society can only be renewed when people are renewed, and people can only be renewed by a personal faith-relationship to the Renewer which necessarily results in a pledged loyalty to the Lordship of the Renewer.

RESENTMENT

1224. If you hug to yourself any resentment against anybody else, you destroy the bridge by which God would come to you.

Peter Marshall

1225. Those who say they will forgive but can't forget, simply bury the hatchet, but they leave the handle out for immediate use.

Dwight L. Moody

RESISTANCE TO EVIL

(See: Christian Action.)

RESPONSIBILITY

1226. Whatever your lot in life, build something on it.

1227. He who feels no responsibility to a higher power feels no responsibility.

REVENGE

1228. Revenge is the most worthless weapon in the world. It ruins the avenger while more firmly confirming the enemy in his wrong. It initiates an endless flight down a bottomless stairway of rancorous reprisals and ruthless retaliations.

David Augsburger

REVIVAL

1229. Revival means being brought to our original condition when we first met the Lord.

Melva Wickman

1230. The revivals of the church have commonly been due to a sudden consciousness that Jesus Christ has been forgotten or undervalued in the very church which bore His name.

James Moffatt

1231. Some say revivals don't last. Neither does a bath, but it's helpful.

Billy Sunday

1232. Revival is nothing else than a new beginning of obedience to God.

Charles G. Finney

1233. True revival has always begun with and resulted in separation.
Vernon Patterson

1234. When revival comes it does not unite incompatibles, it separates them irrevocably.
William E. Hill

S

SALVATION

1235. To say that one may still be a believer in Christ and live in direct disobedience to His will is to take mental assent for saving faith. In that case, to believe "Christ died for my sins" makes no more difference than to believe that "water is H_2O."

W. T. Purkiser

1236. The Bible reports on one deathbed repentance, so that none need despair. But only one, so that none need presume.

Saint Augustine

1237. I have never met a man who thought he had his sins forgiven, unless it was through the blood of Christ.

Cecil Burridge

1238. If you never know me, you will miss nothing. But if you never know Him whom I serve, you will miss everything.

1239. We are not saved by sincerity but we may certainly be lost through insincerity.

Robert Black

1240. You can have what you need—now! And when you have what you most need, you'll realize it is also what you most want.

1241. Salvation is a free gift. And if it's free, I can't earn it or improve upon it [not even] if I live to be 1,000 and learn to preach like Billy Graham

Phyllis K. Miller

1242. A number of years ago, "Ripley's Believe It Or Not" told of a London lawyer, Fred Charington, who refused an inheritance of five million dollars. He asked permission of the court to decline an inheritance of five million dollars! The spiritual counterpart to this is not as immediately staggering, but infinitely more consequential.

1243. I remember two things: that I am a great sinner and that Christ is a great Saviour.

John Newton

(See also: Conversion; New Birth.)

SANCTIFICATION

1244. [Sanctification] is the work of God's free grace, whereby we are renewed in the whole man after the image of God, and are enabled more and more to die unto sin, and live unto righteousness.

Westminster Shorter Catechism

(See also: Holiness.)

SCIENCE

1245. No life per se has been isolated. Because of the threshold's vanishing, those chemists who are preoccupied in synthesizing the particular atomically structured molecules identified as the prime constituents of humanly employed organisms, if chemically successful, will be as remote from creating life as are automobile manufacturers from creating drivers of their automobiles.

R. Buckminster Fuller

SECOND COMING OF CHRIST

1246. According to Kenneth E. Boulding, the greatest dilemma of mankind is that all knowledge is about the past and all decisions are about the future. That's a very clever conclusion which has a nice ring to it. But all knowledge for the Christian is not about the past.

1247. Far too often we have our churches looking for signs while Scripture enjoins the believer to look for the Lord Himself.

Lonnie Gable

SECULARISM

1248. Having bent over backwards to separate church and state in lower schools and maintain academic freedom in higher education, modern man has filled the value vacuum with secular religion. Its creed is: man is God; reason is truth; values are relative; and means are ends.

David L. McKenna

1249. A secular society is one which is organized as if God didn't exist.

Georgia Harkness

1250. While the Bible teaches that experience is important, secular man teaches that experience is paramount.

1251. Modern man has jettisoned all religious substance and is left only with a greater love for his own children than for others. But what does he do if his own children display imperfection?

SECURITY

1252. Security is not the absence of danger, but the presence of God no matter what the danger.

SELF-DENIAL

1253. A man is rich in proportion to the number of things he can afford to let alone.

Henry David Thoreau

1254. Our degree of "resurrection power" is in direct ratio to our involvement in being crucified with Christ.

1255. The concept of resurrection is welcomed by all, but the prior concern of self-crucifixion is a higher price than most men are willing to pay.

1256. God does not want us to think less of ourselves. He wants us not to think of ourselves at all.

Andrew Dhuse

1257. The Christian faith has not been tried and found wanting. It has been found difficult and left untried.

G. K. Chesterton

1258. If to serve God meant unfailing prosperity and unruffled serenity, then people would serve God for none but selfish reasons. But discipleship is more than "decidedship"—Christian discipleship includes staying power.

1259. Life offers only two alternatives: crucifixion with Christ or self-destruction without Him .

1260. The worship of God is always conspicious for its negation of self, for when self is not negated, it is necessarily worshiped.

1261. Few today in the church—almost none in politics—are studying how to be little in their own eyes so they can become great in the [self-denying] service of God.

George E. Failing

1262. As Tertullian said, in the early centuries after Christ, Christianity spread because Christians outlived, outloved, and outdied the pagans.

1263. God will not look you over for medals, degrees, or diplomas, but for scars.

Elbert Hubbard

1264. God is looking for some wicks to burn. The oil and the fire are free.

Hudson Taylor

1265. As a Christian, necessarily and absolutely opposed to the hedonistic spirit of the world, how much rejection can you take? Everything up to and including physical crucifixion?

1266. You deny Christ when you fail to deny yourself for Christ.

1267. "Crucified" is the only really definitive adjective by which to describe the Christian life.

J. Furman Miller

1268. All great virtues bear the imprint of self-denial.

William E. Channing

1269. Teach us, good Lord, to serve Thee as Thou deservest; to give and not count the cost; to fight and not to heed the wounds; to toil and not to seek for rest; to labor and not to ask for any reward, save that of knowing that we do Thy will.

Saint Ignatius of Loyola

(See also: Surrender.)

SELF-EXAMINATION

1270. Too many Christians have lived exceedingly long on the right side of Easter but on the wrong side of Pentecost; on the right side of forgiveness, but on the wrong side of fellowship; on the right side of pardon, but on the wrong side of power.

Alan Redpath

1271. Do we find it easier to go to church than to be the church?

1272. The earth is worth our salt—are we?

Kenneth L. Wilson

1273. Everybody thinks of changing humanity and nobody thinks of changing himself.

Leo Tolstoy

1274. When we, like Adam and Eve, have undergone the shock of self-discovery, we are likewise ashamed of what we see.

Keith Huttenlocker

1275. In judging of others a man labors in vain, often errs, and easily sins, but in judging and examining himself, he always labors fruitfully.

Thomas a Kempis

SELF-PITY

1276. Self-pity is a prison without walls—a sign pointing to nowhere.

SEPARATION

1277. If the church maintains her separation from the world, she will always be despised. If she ever becomes popular, it will be a sign of compromise.

Reuel G. Lemmons

1278. When the line separating citizenship of this world with citizenship of the heavenly kingdom is blurred or removed, the church is soon in trouble.

Joseph Bayly

1279. There are no traffic jams on the straight and narrow way.

1280. True revival has always begun with and resulted in separation.

Vernon Patterson

1281. People around us may not accept our faith; but they do expect professing Christians to be different as, indeed, they should be.

1282. I need to know how people of the Devil's domain live. But I don't need to know badly enough to continually heap their garbage on my dinner table.

W. T. Purkiser

1283. It is impossible for the purity of the Christian and the pollution of the pagan to run in double harness.

William Barclay

SERVICE

1284. The greatest among men is always ready to serve and yet is unconscious of the service.

Helena P. Blavatsky

1285. God owns no slaves. All His people serve Him because they want to. What's more, they find unspeakable joy in so doing.

1286. Service in the Christian sense is almost always sacrificial in character. It's not a question of waiting for a surplus in order to give. Service means giving life itself, or in Pauline terms, spending oneself for Christ.
Samuel Escobar

1287. Make us masters of ourselves that we may be the servants of others.
Sir Alexander Paterson

1288. How far that candle throws his beams,
   So shines a good deed in a naughty world.
William Shakespeare

1289. God breaks up the private life of His saints and makes it a thoroughfare for the world. No one can stand that unless he is identified with Christ.... Let God make you broken bread and poured out wine in His hand for others.
Oswald Chambers

1290. No load is irksome that is voluntarily assumed. It is compulsion that destroys.

1291. Christians are called to serve—but we are not called to serve the unregenerate desires of people.

1292. Rules or commandments are not so much a formula for faith as they are a descriptive account of what takes place when creature and Creator are related to each other in love. The same may also be said for social action and Christian service.

1293. Good deeds are not good if they stop short of introducing a person to the highest good of all, the lordship of Jesus Christ.
Myron Augsburger

1294. You must live with people to know their problems, and live with God in order to solve them.
Peter T. Forsyth

1295. He who labors as he prays lifts his heart to God with his hands.
Saint Bernard of Clairvaux

1296. Do all the good you can, in all the ways you can, to all the people you can, as long as ever you can.
John Wesley

1297. To be His slave is to be a king.

William Barclay

(See also: Christian Action.)

SEX

1298. The Christian church says to every bridegroom: "Through this woman you are to explore the whole of womankind. If you turn elsewhere, seeking more, you will in fact find less." And this principle applies equally to the bride.

1299. What happens when sex is liberated is not equality but a vast intensification of sexual competition from which there is no sure haven except impotence and defeat; competition in which marriage is just another arena, or the home base from which the strong deploy; competition in which the only sure result is an ever larger band of vindictive losers.

George Gilder

1300. Abortions are performed by the thousands simply because people want the freedom of promiscuous sex but not the responsibility of children.

R. Eugene Sterner

1301. In a world of mass murder and mass starvation, of unprecedented terror, odious tyrannies and the threat of nuclear holocausts—in such a world there is something obscene about an order of priorities that starts off with bigger and better orgasms.

Peter L. Berger

1302. In man, illicit sex is the effort of the flesh to rape the spirit. Only spiritual strength can successfully resist this attack.

1303. Those who devote themselves to the exclusive pursuit of sexual happiness are not apt to find it.

Alfred Gross

1304. The sex experience between spouses is only creative and psychologically productive when it is at the same time both self-searching and self-giving. This level of experience is seldom embraced because it only comes at that point when the egos mutually put down their defenses.

SHARING

1305. It is easy enough to tell the poor to accept their

poverty as God's will when you yourself have warm clothes and plenty of food and medical care and a roof over your head and no worry about the rent. But if you want them to believe you—try to share some of their poverty and see if you can accept it as God's will yourself.

Thomas Merton

1306. The earth provides enough for every man's need but not for every man's greed.

Mahatma Gandhi

1307. We make a living by what we get—a life by what we give.

(See also: Charity; Stewardship.)

SIMPLICITY

1308. Amish people lead a simple life with less stress. Perhaps they have learned their limitations as humans. It may be that man's horse-and-buggy nervous system cannot cope with today's jet-propelled, supersonic, nonstop, pill-popping pace.

SIN

1309. The heart of the problem is a problem of the heart.

1310. When we, like Adam and Eve, have undergone the shock of self-discovery, we are likewise ashamed of what we see.

Keith Huttenlocker

1311. The greatest sin is to be concious of none.

1312. Satan is the Santa Claus of sin. He has "toys" for everyone.

1313. Sin would have few takers if its consequences always occurred immediately.

1314. Sin is something like putting on weight. Most people don't worry too much about it, until it starts making them look bad.

Sylvia Doolin

1315.   Vice is a monster of such frightful mien,
As, to be hated, needs but to be seen.
But seen too oft, familiar with her face,
We first endure, then pity, then embrace.

Alexander Pope

1316. More persons are ready to shrink from sinners than are ready to shrink from sin.

1317. Those who stray from paths of righteousness may find God's forgiveness, but only eternity heals the scars.
Joel Danner

1318. All the old primitive sins are not dead, but are crouching in the dark corners of our modern hearts.
Carl G. Jung

1319. The wages of sin have never been reduced.

1320. There's nothing wrong in this world except for sin.
C. M. Ward

1321. Anytime you live it up, you run the risk of having to live it down.

1322. Sin is the willful continuation of a fractured relationship with God.

1323. Whatever weakens your reason, impairs the tenderness of your conscience, obscures your sense of God, or takes off your relish for spiritual things—that is sin to you.
Susannah Wesley

1324. An uncontrolled appetite in the presence of correct light signifies an uncontrolled heart.
Thomas Doty

1325. It is of the heart of sin that men use what they ought to enjoy and enjoy what they ought to use.
Saint Augustine

SOCIAL GOSPEL

1326. The individual-salvation gospel always carries with it social concern. But the social gospel seldom possesses spiritual substance.

1327. Any social action program that does not give priority to a spiritual ministry is, however unwittingly, merely financing the damning designs of Satan.

1328. The desire for social reform often stems from religious concern. But one can be religiously motivated without being God oriented, in which case, social concern will be void of lasting redemptive value.

1329. If a surgeon operated on a patient for acute appendicitis and left the appendix in, he would be sued for malpractice and fraud. But when a minister preaches to lost men a social gospel which cannot save—well, he may be made a bishop.
L. Nelson Bell

1330. Show me a man who fears God, who trembles before divine judgment, and who is preoccupied in this life with preparing for the next; and I'll show you a man who is living a life which is relevant and productive for the here-and-now.

1331. Every major revival has had in its wake more social improvement than a thousand meetings called specifically for social action.

1332. When we want twice-born men as much as we want social justice, we will find both.

1333. We must not confuse the aim of Christian mission with the results.

1334. Reformation which springs from any source other than regeneration washes only the outside of the cup.

L. Nelson Bell

SOCIALISM

1335. Socialism will work only in two places: in heaven where it's not needed, and in hell where they already have it. Capitalism is the unequal distribution of wealth. Socialism is the equal distribution of poverty. Communism is nothing but socialism with a gun at your back.

Winston Churchill

1336. Society cannot leap into Communism from capitalism without going through a socialist stage of development. Socialism is the first stage to Communism.

Nikita S. Khrushchev

1337. The main objection a socialist has to capital is that he hasn't any.

Wes Izzard

1338. I'm against a homogenized society because I want the cream to rise.

Robert Frost

STEWARDSHIP

1339. Arrogant giving can turn the best of gifts to ashes.

Kenneth L. Wilson

1340. Americans often spend more than they make on things they don't need to impress people they don't like.

1341. American men and women spend 18 per cent

more on cosmetic products and services than on all religious and welfare activities combined. Many Christians spend more for cosmetics than they give to world missions. And when they stand before the Judgment Seat of Christ to give an account of their lives (I Corinthians 3), how will they explain the imbalance?

1342. When we assume responsibility for God's concerns, He assumes responsibility for our needs.
Roberta Bonnici

1343. Have you ever heard anyone say that he suffered because he tithed?

1344. He who needs least is most like the gods.
Socrates

1345. The worth of a person's gift to God is determined more by what is left than by the amount given.

1346. You can give without loving—but you can't love without giving.

1347. The cure for the problems of affluence is not poverty. It is stewardship.

1348. What I spent, I had. What I kept, I lost. What I gave, I have.

(See also: Charity; Time.)

STRENGTH

1349. The strength and happiness of a man consists in finding out the way in which God is going, and going in that way too.
Henry Ward Beecher

SUCCESS

1350. Every man who is happily married is a successful man, even if he has failed in everything else.
William Lyon Phelps

1351. Better to attempt something great and fail than to attempt something small and succeed.

1352. A great many people go through life in bondage to success. They are in mortal dread of failure. I do not have to succeed. I have only to be true to the highest I know—success or failure are in the hands of God.
E. Stanley Jones

1353. A man can do only what he can do. But if he does that each day he can sleep at night and do it again the next day.
Albert Schweitzer

1354. The secret of success is constancy of purpose.
Benjamin Disraeli

1355. It takes twenty years to be an overnight success.
Eddie Cantor

1356. Success means getting up one more time than you fall down.

1357. Success is not the issue. How much you pay for it is.

Keith Huttenlocker

1358. Success is finding or making that position which enables you to contribute to the world the very greatest service of which you are capable, through the diligent, persevering, resolute cultivation of all the faculties God has endowed you with, and doing it with all cheerfulness, scorning to allow difficulties or defeats to drive you to pessimism or despair.

B. C. Forbes

1359. Before everything else, getting ready is the secret of success.

Henry Ford

1360. Men who are afraid of being ruined by success should get a job with the weather bureau.

1361. Real success is having courage to meet failure without being defeated.

SUFFERING

1362. A Christian is someone who shares the sufferings of God in the world.

Dietrich Bonhoeffer

1363. I know that God is not going to willfully hurt us. Why there is suffering is the business of the Lord, but He never seems to give us any more than we can bear.

Martin Luther King, Sr.

1364. Know how sublime a thing it is to suffer and be strong.

Henry Wadsworth Longfellow

1365. God does not mock His children with a night that has no ending; and to every man who stands resolute while the darkness lasts, there comes at length the vindication of faith and the breaking of the day.

James S. Stewart

1366. We are not in this world simply to enjoy God's

gifts. We are here to use them in the building of His kingdom, which calls for some kind of suffering.
Arnold G. Kuntz

1367. It is not miserable to be blind; it is miserable to be incapable of enduring blindness.
John Milton

1368. The heavenly Father has no spoiled children. He loves them too much to allow that.
Fred Mitchell

1369. Look upon your chastenings as God's chariots sent to carry your soul into the high places of spiritual achievement.
Hannah Whithall Smith

1370. The strangest truth of the Gospel is that redemption comes through suffering.
Milo L. Chapman

(See also: Trouble.)

SUNDAY

1371. If you want to kill Christianity, you must abolish Sunday.
Voltaire

SURRENDER

1372. We attempt to be the "person" people think we ought to be, but that person is often not the person we think we are. The only way to bring practical order out of this personal chaos is to be the person God wants us to be.

1373. Before we can pray, "Lord, Thy Kingdom come," we must be willing to pray, "My kingdom go."
Alan Redpath

1374. The altar is not a bargain counter where you haggle with God. It is a peace table where you agree to unconditional surrender.

1375. When you mortgage what is right, only Christ can buy it back. Only Christ can purchase your redemption. But His fee is high. Not in dollars and cents. It doesn't cost money. Spiritual freedom costs more than money. It will cost you your life.

1376. You must die while you live before you can live after you die.

1377. If you don't surrender to Christ, you surrender to chaos.

E. Stanley Jones

1378. God will only mend a broken heart when He is given all the pieces.

(See also: Commitment; Self-denial.)

T

TELEVISION

1379. With the advent of television, people no longer have a good time—they watch a good time.

1380. All television is educational television. The only question is, what is it teaching?

Nicholas Johnson

1381. There is no such thing as politically neutral entertainment.

Herbert I. Schiller

1382. The average eighteen-year-old American has seen eighteen thousand hours of TV.

Neil P. Hurley

1383. A television-repair advertisement read: "We can fix anything wrong with your TV set except the lousy programs."

1384. The indiscriminate viewing of television has done more to destroy the home, decrease the influence of the church, and despiritualize Christians than any other single force in our time.

1385. Two things that have been said about religion can also be said about television: that it is the opiate of the masses, and that it can inspire truth, goodness and beauty, or mendacity, viciousness and evil.

Robert Liebert

1386. A family watching television is a way of doing nothing together.

TEMPERANCE

1387. The only temperance which has any value . . . has its source, not in scanty supply, but in strong self-restraint.

TEMPTATION

1388. The human race began in a garden—a wonderful world in which there was only one forbidden fruit. Because we fell victim to a single prohibition, we must now walk through a world which hangs heavy with forbidden fruit. And our forward progress is unceasingly impeded by an ever increasing crop of enticing fruit trees loaded with spiritual poison.

1389. Calling on Jesus to help you overcome temptation may look weak to men. But the demons know it is their undoing.

1390. People do not decide to be drunkards, drug addicts, prostitutes, murderers or thieves, but they pitch their tent toward Sodom and the powers of evil overcome them.

John H. Eastwood

1391. Temptation wins its easiest victories over those whose hearts are restless and dissatisfied because the issue of their ultimate loyalty has never been fully settled.

W. T. Purkiser

1392. All he [Satan] needs to do is lead us quietly astray, off the straight and narrow path of righteousness. If he leads us but one or two degrees off that path, well-planned rationalization will soon silence our critics and we can rest secure in the fact that we are still very close to truth and right.

Norman De Jong

1393. Flirting with temptation is never innocent for the Christian. There is just one thing to do when temptation rears its beautiful and lovely head—*fight*!

THANKSGIVING

1394. Not what we say about our blessings but how we use them is the true measure of our thanksgiving.

W. T. Purkiser

1395. Whenever a man finds nothing to be thankful for, that man has to reach up to touch bottom.

1396. Thanksgiving is a duty before it is a feeling.

C. M. Ward

1397. The man who forgets to be grateful has fallen asleep in life.

Robert Louis Stevenson

1398. Measuring God's love by material blessings alone is like trying to drive a car with nothing but dirty water in the gas tank. Praise which extends only from prosperity is closer to idolatry than thankfulness.

1399. For all that has been—thanks! To all that shall be—yes!
Dag Hammarskjold

1400. On the night Matthew Henry was robbed he prayed: "I thank Thee first because I was never robbed before; second, because although they took my purse they did not take my life; third, although they took my all, it was not much; and fourth, because it was I who was robbed and not I who robbed."

(See also: Praise.)

THEOLOGY

1401. Theology teaches us what ends are desirable and what means are lawful, while politics teaches what means are effective.
C. S. Lewis

1402. My entire theology can be condensed into four words: "Jesus died for me."
Charles Spurgeon

1403. The ultimate home of radical theology is Marxism.
Billy Graham

1404. A whole generation of religious thinkers is busy cutting itself loose from history and tradition and casting away both the forms and faith they consider too old to be valid.

THOUGHT

1405. The reason there are so few good talkers in public is that there are so few good thinkers in private.
(See also: The Mind.)

TIME

1406. Time is the deposit each one has in the bank of God and no one knows the balance.
Ralph W. Sockman

1407. As if you could kill time without injuring eternity.
Henry David Thoreau

1408. Time is a three-fold present: the present as we experience it, the past as a present memory, and the future as a present expectation.

Saint Augustine

1409. I have only just a minute,
Just sixty seconds in it;
Forced upon me—can't refuse it,
Didn't seek it; didn't choose it;
I must suffer if I lose it,
Give account if I abuse it;
Just a tiny little minute,
But eternity is in it.

1410. The chief end of man is to sanctify time. All it takes to sanctify time is God, a soul, and a moment. And the three are always here.

Abraham J. Heschel

1411. Yesterday is already a dream and tomorrow is only a vision. But today, well lived, makes every yesterday a dream of happiness and every tomorrow a vision of hope.

The Koran

1412. Time goes, you say? Ah, no! Alas, time stays, we go!

Henry A. Dobson

1413. No time for God?
What fools we are . . .
No time for God?
As soon to say no time
To eat, to sleep, to live, to die.
Take time for God,
Or a poor misshapen thing you'll be
To step into eternity,
And say,
"I had no time for Thee."

(See also: The Future; History; The New Year; The Past; The Present.)

TRIBULATION

(See: Suffering; Trouble.)

TROUBLE

1414. At the profoundest depths in life, men talk not about God, but with Him.

D. Elton Trueblood

1415. Battles are really won in the preparation effort made for them.
W. T. Purkiser

1416. Those who have a "why" to live, can bear with almost any "how."
Victor E. Frankl

1417. What the individual does with a calamity or a bad break usually determines what he'll do with his life.
Norman Vincent Peale

1418. The only adequate response [to God] is faith and trust, never the search for satisfaction itself.
Richard E. Wentz

1419. The bitterest cup with Christ is better than the sweetest cup without Him.
Ian MacPherson

1420. Sorrow touched by love grows bright,
   With more than rapture's ray;
   And darkness shows us worlds of light
   We never saw by day.

1421. If we really believe God, we would welcome the chance to come to grips with problems. But alas, we are like the little girl who wrote her aunt a thank-you note: "Dear Aunt Harriet: Thank you for the pin-cushion you sent me for my birthday. I always wanted a pin-cushion, but not very much."
Ethel Barrett

1422. My soul, thou art receiving a music lesson from thy Father. Thou art being educated for the choir invisible. There are parts in the symphony that none can take but thee. Thy Father is training thee for the part the angels cannot sing, and the school is sorrow. In the night He is preparing thy song. In the valley He is tuning thy voice. In the cloud He is deepening thy chords. In the rain He is sweetening thy melody. In the cold He is molding thy expression. Despise not the school of sorrow.
George Matheson

1423. Adversity does not make us frail; it only shows us how frail we are.

1424. If you make a bad bargain, hug it all the tighter.
Abraham Lincoln

1425. It is wonderful what God can do with the broken heart, if He gets all the pieces.

1426. If our circumstances find us in God, we shall find God in our circumstances.

George Mueller

1427. For every evil under the sun
There is a remedy or there is none.
If there be one, seek to find it;
If there be none, never mind it.

1428. Where there are no trials in life there are no triumphs.

1429. The school of faith teaches us to trust God to solve our problems. And then, for a graduate course, it teaches us to trust God when He chooses not to solve our problems.

Stephen Board

1430. The agony of a man's affliction is often necessary to put him into the right mood to face the fundamental things of life. The Psalmist says: "Before I was afflicted I went astray, but now have I kept Thy word."

Oswald Chambers

1431. The total absence of problems would be the beginning of death for a society or an individual. We are not fitted to live in a problemless world. This is so much the case that when the problems of the real world are not pressing in upon us, we invent artificial problems such as lowering our golf score.

1432. Scientific progress as a solution to human problems is a blind alley. For the more efficient and self-sufficient we become, the less our sense of dependency on God, and, therefore, the farther removed we are from Him. It is often the problems of human experience that move us toward God.

1433. The hammer shatters glass, but forges steel.

1434. A full and complete reading of the New Testament will show conclusively that God has not promised to solve our problems or answer our questions or melt away our tribulations. If we can ever get our sense of values in proper Christian focus, we will come to understand that the loving presence of God in the trial furnace is a far greater blessing than the elimination of trouble by divine intervention.

1435. Nothing influences the quality of our life more than how we respond to trouble.

Erwin G. Tieman

1436. Receive every inward and outward trouble, every disappointment, pain, uneasiness, temptation, darkness and desolation with both hands, as to a true opportunity and blessed occasion of dying to self and entering into a fuller fellowship with thy self-denying suffering Savior.
John Wesley

1437. Mishaps are knives that either serve us or cut us as we grasp them by the blade or by the handle.
James Russell Lowell

1438. Obstacles are those frightening things you see when you take your eyes off your goal.

1439. We may not be responsible for all the things that happen to us, but we are responsible for the way we behave when they do happen.

1440. The pessimist says of trouble: "It's enough to make a person lose his religion," while the optimist says: "It's enough to make a person use his religion."

1441. No life meaningfully linked to God can be utterly cast down.

1442. But in the mud and scum of things,
 There alway, alway something sings.
Ralph Waldo Emerson

1443. If you keep within your heart a green branch, I have heard there will come one day a singing bird.

1444. Everything that happens to me can help me along in my Christian life.
E. Stanley Jones

1445. What we call adversity, God calls opportunity. What we call tribulation, God calls growth.

(See also: Suffering.)

TRUST

1446. Security is not the absence of danger, but the presence of God no matter what the danger.

1447. The school of faith teaches us to trust God to solve our problems. And then, for a graduate course, it teaches us to trust God when He chooses not to solve our problems.
Stephen Board

1448. Only when we have enough mental stress to force us to see our own bankruptcy of power, do we trust in

God, and only when we trust in God can we make a contribution which will not collapse.

Kenneth L. Pike

(See also: Faith.)

TRUSTWORTHINESS

1449. This above all: to thine own self be true.
And it must follow as the night the day,
Thou canst not then be false to any man.

William Shakespeare

TRUTH

1450. Plato, three hundred years before Christ, predicted that if ever the truly good man were to appear, the man who would tell the truth, he would have his eyes gouged out and in the end be crucified. That risk was once taken, in its fullest measure. The Man appeared. He told the world the truth—about itself—and even made the preposterous claim: "I am the Truth." As Plato foresaw, that Man was crucified.

Elisabeth Elliot

1451. What men commonly call love is usually an affectation which shuns like the plague truth between people. Where there is no will to truth, even sacrifice turns to flattery.

Knud E. Logstrup

1452. If truth isn't revealed by God, then it's invented by men. And if it's invented, then one man's "truth" is as good as another's. And if one man's truth is as good as another's, then the inevitable result is absolute anarchy.

1453. The Devil tries to shake truth by pretending to defend it.

Tertullian

1454. It is possible to know "all the answers" without knowing Him who is the answer.

Vance Havner

1455. Every man has a right to his opinion, but his opinion may not be right.

Arthur H. Townsend

1456. Truth is more often imagined to be spontaneously generated by passion than patiently discovered by reason.

Calvin D. Linton

1457. Truth must triumph. All else is expendable.

1458. Though love repine, and reason chafe,
   There came a voice without reply—
   'Tis man's perdition to be safe,
   When for the truth he ought to die.
   Ralph Waldo Emerson

1459. From the apathy that is satisfied with unimportant truth, from the cowardice that shrinks from new truth, from the laziness that is content with half-truths, and from the arrogance that thinks it knows all the truth, O God of Truth, deliver us.

1460. Every man has a right to his opinion, but no man has a right to be wrong in his facts.
   Bernard M. Baruch

1461. Our first love must be love of truth. Cooperation based on sentiment alone is not cooperation of any value; it is merely organizational insanity.
   David Breese

1462. The number of people who believe a thing to be true does not even create a presumption about it one way or the other.
   William G. Sumner

1463. Human kind cannot bear very much reality [truth].
   T. S. Eliot

1464. Agnosticism doubts truth. Rationalism questions truth. Infidelity scoffs at truth. Logic dissects truth. Education searches for truth. But Jesus said: "I am the truth."

1465. Hear the just law, the judgment of the skies,
   He that hates the truth shall be the dupe of lies;
   And he that will be cheated to the last,
   Delusions strong as hell shall bind him fast.
   William Cowper

1466. Truth is always narrow, but error goes off in all directions.
   Paul E. Johnson

1467. In John Godfrey Saxe's *The Blind Men and the Elephant*, each man reached out to touch that part of the elephant nearest to him. From this touch, each one conceived his image of the whole. Thus, the elephant's side suggested a wall, the tusk a spear, the trunk a snake, the knee a tree, the ear a fan, and the tail a rope. So the poet concludes:

> And so these men of Indostan
> Disputed loud and long;
> Each in his own opinion,
> Exceeding stiff and strong.
> Though each was partly in the right,
> They all were in the wrong.

1468. Persons and groups who are almost but not absolutely right, are far more dangerous than the open adversaries who are wholly wrong.

Rose Wilder Lane

1469. Truth does not change according to season or place. For it is not of man but of eternal God.

Yang Won Son

TYRANNY

1470. Civilization is always in danger when those who have never learned to obey are given the right to command.

Fulton J. Sheen

U

UNITED STATES

1471. America will never be turned to God by simply permitting people to pray. But no nation will long endure when it is the law that one is forbidden to pray in school or on other public property.

(See also: The Nation; United States—Moral Climate.)

UNITED STATES—MORAL CLIMATE

1472. Extremism which we see today in the arts, in custom, in morals, in religion, in dress and in relations between the sexes is all practiced in the name of freedom. But this extremism is the harbinger of tyranny which is even now hacking away at the foundation of our republic.

1473. I used to say that civilization was going to the dogs. But I've quit saying that out of respect for the dogs.

Vance Havner

1474. The American dream will end when the American people fall asleep, as surely as other dreams end when people wake up.

J. Kesner Kahn

1475. The reason we have a society of moral runaways is quite simple. Few firm and particular moral guidelines have been set forth or enforced by preachers or parents. The Bible provides us with specific moral absolutes; but the golden goddess of education lured us with an enticing freedom of the flesh, predicated, logically enough, on "theories of relativity" pregnant with new moralities and situation ethics. The goddess of education then gleefully played the role of midwife and delivered the destructive and depraved social demons of humanism and hedonism which are now stalking our nation toward a self-destruction—not relative but absolute.

1476. We have so many laws because we are a lawless people. Why else would we need so many laws?

1477. We have now sunk to a depth at which the restatement of the obvious is the first duty of intelligent men.

George Orwell

1478. Young people today are either being taught the wrong values or not being taught the right ones. So given this circumstance, the degeneration of society will continue, if not by design, then by default.

1479. In 1857 an English historian, Thomas B. Macaulay, wrote about the U.S.: "Your republic will be fearfully plundered and laid waste by barbarians in the twentieth century as the Roman Empire was in the fifth century—with this difference: that the Huns and Vandals who ravaged the Roman Empire came from without but your Huns and Vandals will have been engendered within your own country by your own institutions."

1480. You cannot at once both love God with all your heart and lust after pleasure and plenty.

1481. We live in an age of nuclear giants and spiritual dwarfs.

Omar N. Bradley

1482. The emphasis today is not on what is principled but on what is popular, not on what is functional but on what is fashionable, and not on how much we construct but on how much we consume.

1483. If the new Christian left has its way, power will become our god, conflict our christ, and contempt our unholy ghost.

1484. If God doesn't punish our modern world for its immoral excesses, He will have to apologize to Sodom and Gomorrah.

Billy Graham

UNITY

1485. Unity is only as good as the direction toward which it is aimed. Disunity has often been a blessing to foil evil intent. And, by the same token, unity has been a curse in giving strength to unholy purpose.

1486. Better to shun "unity for its own sake" than to sink with a loser because you stayed with a loser.

1487. Unity must be according to God's Holy Word, or else it were better war than peace.

Hugh Latimer

1488. There is one thing worse than a church division and that is an unchecked slide into apostasy. Unless unity be according to God's Word, better conflict than calm.

1489. Some unity is like two cats tied by their tails and thrown across the clothesline.

V

VALUES

1490. It is easy to lose what really matters in life because we are paying attention to what merely matters most often.

1491. Good is not good where better is expected.

Thomas Fuller

1492. Aim at heaven and you get earth thrown in. Aim at earth and you get neither.

C. S. Lewis

VICTORY

1493. Your outcome in life doesn't depend on your income, but on how you overcome.

1494. May God deny you peace, but give you glory.

Miguel de Unamuno

1495. Great supplicants have sought the secret place of the Most High, not that they might escape the world, but that they might learn to conquer it.

Samuel Chadwick

1496. If life is a comedy to him who thinks, and a tragedy to him who feels, it is a victory to him who believes.

VISION

1497. The Christians who have turned the world upside down have been men and women with a vision in their hearts, and the Bible in their hands.

T. B. Maston

W

WAR

1498. An old Judean proverb states: "Resistance to tyranny is the highest obedience to God."

1499. Sometimes the brutality of one's enemies requires a counter-violence—this is the principle of self-defense and the just war.

1500. The only men who do not serve in some army are those who are ruled by someone else's army. Without power you must do as you are told. When you lay down your arms, it's not the saints who will come marching in.

1501. The Vietnam War was one which Americans were afraid to win and ashamed to lose.

Paul Harvey

1502. Sixty-five wars have been fought since the U.N. was first formed—that's a new war every six months.

1503. Saying we will end a war by withdrawing our troops is no less naive than saying we will end crime by withdrawing the officers of law enforcement.

1504. The only immorality about the war in Vietnam is that we failed to do in ten years what we should have done in ten days—and this dismal failure needlessly cost us fifty thousand American lives.

1505. The teaching of the Sermon on the Mount is a personal ethic of Christian faith and obedience to law, to be practiced by a Christian toward peers. It does not apply to relationships of nations except that in the process of stopping by force the unreasonable and inhuman acts of another nation, a "best interest" love is well served and explicitly expressed. Self-defense in no way presupposes hate.

WEAKNESS

1506. There are two ways to be as weak and soft as a wet dishtowel. One is by not having strong convictions. The other is by holding one's convictions in isolation from the reality they were meant to change.

John Vriend

WISDOM

1507. An illiterate wise man is not half so dangerous as an educated fool.

1508. Common sense is not always Christian and Christian sense is seldom common.

1509. A wise man will learn from the mistakes of others. Because, after all, there isn't time for him to make all of them himself.

1510. Every man is a fool for five minutes out of every day, and wisdom consists in not exceeding that limit.

Elbert Hubbard

1511. Those who cannot remember the past are condemned to repeat it.

George Santayana

1512. The only wisdom we can hope to acquire is the wisdom of humility—humility is endless.

T. S. Eliot

1513. The wise learn from tragedy; the foolish merely repeat it.

Michael Novak

WITNESSING

(See: Christian Witness.)

WOMEN

1514. Dear Women's Libber: If you wish not to be thought of as a sex symbol, stop dressing like one.

1515. A lady is a woman who makes a man behave like a gentleman.

Russell Lynes

1516. When the worldly women decided to appear less modest by hiking up their hemlines, why did church women follow suit? To glorify Christ or to worship at the beloved altar of conformity?

1517. Having a family doesn't guarantee a woman freedom and fulfillment, but it does offer endless oppor-

tunity for practicing those disciplines necessary for personal growth which lead to enrichment and fulfillment.
LaVerna Klippenstein

1518. Trying to bring women down and make them equal with men is sort of like putting mud in ice cream. It doesn't help the mud and it ruins the ice cream.
Chub Seawell

1519. The most important occupation on earth for a woman is to be a real mother to her children. It does not have much glory to it; there is a lot of grit and grime. But there is no greater place of ministry, position or power than that of a mother.
Phil Whisenhunt

1520. If women wish to be treated more as persons and less as sex objects, they should emphasize personality over sexuality by wearing less revealing clothing.

WOMEN'S LIBERATION

(See: Women.)

WORK

(See: Labor.)

WORLDLINESS

1521. I warn and charge you from the Lord not to make any of the world's jewels your God.
George Fox

1522. When silly furors and fashions rage, the chaff in our churches always goes with the gale.
Theodore L. Cuyler

1523. Friendship with the world is any attempt on the part of the believer to hide the fact of his true identity.
Timothy F. Merrill

1524. There is a worldly secular gospel that is a popular mixture of Christianity, worldliness, and the notion that we can at the same time be both Christians and worldlings. Yet a friend of the world is an enemy with God.
Vance Havner

1525. If the church insists on looking like the world, dressing like the world, acting like the world, and living like the world, it will be difficult to convince the worldling that we have anything to offer which he doesn't already have in greater abundance.

1526. We are all earthlings, but only those who reject Christ are worldlings.

1527. The reason the church has not invaded the world is because the world has invaded the church.

(See also: Materialism and Hedonism.)

WORLD MISSIONS

1528. When Charles Spurgeon was asked whether he thought the heathen, who had never heard the Gospel, could be saved, he replied: "It is more a question with me whether we, who have the Gospel and fail to give it to those who do not, can be saved."

WORRY

1529. The way to worry about nothing is to pray about everything.

1530. Worry is a futile thing,
It's somewhat like a rocking chair.
Although it keeps you occupied,
It doesn't get you anywhere.

F. G. Kernan

1531. A day of worry is more exhausting than a week of work.

John Lubbuck

(See also: Peace of Mind.)

WORSHIP

1532. If you can leave your church on Sunday morning with no feeling of discomfort, of conviction, of brokenness, of challenge, then for you the hour of worship has not been as dangerous as it should have been. The ease with which we go on being Christian sentimentalists is one of our worst faults.

Paul S. Rees

1533. We have become so engrossed in the work of the Lord that we have forgotten the Lord of the work.

A. W. Tozer

1534. The man who does not habitually worship is but a pair of spectacles behind which there is no eye.

Thomas Carlyle

1535. Worship is one thing and entertainment is another, and it is dangerous business to play lightly with holy things, to tickle the senses in place of calling men to bow their hearts in faith and repentance before Him who is Creator and Redeemer of us all.

John C. Neville, Jr.

1536. I'll go where you want me to go, dear Lord,
Over mountain or plain or sea.
But don't ask me to sit in an up-front pew,
That's a little too close for me.

1537. To worship is to quicken the conscience by the holiness of God, to feed the mind with the truth of God, to purge the imagination by the beauty of God, to open the heart to the love of God, to devote the will to the purpose of God.

William Temple

1538. The worship of God is always conspicuous for its negation of self; for when self is not negated, it is necessarily worshiped.

1539. Most Christians tend to worship their work, to work at their play, and to play with their worship.

Gordon Dahl

1540. Carnal men are content with the "act" of worship; they have no desire for communion with God.

John W. Everett

Y

YOUTH

1541. One of the great ironies of our time is a youth culture which forever espouses something they call love—love which somehow fails to include their parents. This is no culture—youth or otherwise. Such a movement is merely a social subgroup gorging itself on self-pity.

1542. Demoralize the youth of a nation and the revolution is already won.

Nikolai Lenin

1543. A high school girl I know of in a Catholic school recently asked her teacher: "But, Sister, what did Christ redeem us from?" This good suburban girl was born and nourished without a sense of evil. There are millions like her, children, not only of affluence but also of untruth, believing in reason and progress and goodness. No wonder the world, sooner or later, shocks them and they grow bitter.

Michael Novak

THE LIGHTER SIDE

1544. Inflation is when you have money to burn but can't afford to buy the matches.

R. Daniel Clark

1545. In matters controversial
My perception's very fine;
I always see both sides of things,
The one that's wrong and mine.

1546. We often shoot at nothing and hit it every time.

1547. Life is easier to take than you'd think. You merely accept the impossible, do without the indispensable and bear the intolerable.

Kathleen Norris

1548. Lincoln once answered a heckler: "My good friend here reminds me of a steamboat that used to run down the river when I was a lad. It had a four-foot boiler and a seven-foot whistle. And every time it whistled, it stopped running."

1549. Husband: "I have a sense of humor—I married her." Wife: "I also have a sense of humor—I'm still living with him."

1550. A committee is often a group of people who keep minutes and waste hours.

1551. An intellectual is often thought of as one who states his opinions as facts, in a style difficult for anyone to understand, and with words unfamiliar to most everyone.

1552. Smile! It improves your face value.

1553. By the time a man gets to greener pastures, he can't climb the fence.

1554. Reliable sources disclose the reason why the Soviets have never placed a man on the moon: they fear he might defect.

Kenneth Robertson

1555. A gossip is one who can give all the details without knowing any of the facts.
Franklin P. Jones

1556. Every time you open your mouth you let men look into your mind.
Bruce Barton

1557. When he's lost in big words
The impression grows,
That he's trying to tell you
More than he knows.

1558. Statistics show that women spend 85 per cent of the consumer dollar, children 15 per cent, and men the rest.
Lucille Goodyear

1559. If you have a pain in the neck, thank God you're not a giraffe.
William Barclay

1560. God surely was a humorist because of the way he made the giraffe, the monkey, the donkey and some of you.
Billy Sunday

1561. James Thurber was once asked, "How's your wife?" His classic answer was: "Compared to what?"

1562. We are told that the weaker sex is really the stronger sex. This is due solely to the weakness of the stronger sex for the weaker sex.

1563. Fat man to skinny man: "You look as if there had been a famine." Skinny man to fat man: "You look as if you caused it."

1564. A duty is a job you try to avoid, perform poorly, and brag about continually.

1565. An economist is a fellow who can tell you tomorrow why what he predicted yesterday didn't happen today.
George Eyer

1566. If your outgo exceeds your income, then your upkeep will be your downfall.

1567. A diehard is a man who worships the ground his head is buried in.

1568. A comfortably filled church is one with enough room in the pews for everyone to lie down and be comfortable.
Ralph W. Sockman

1569. Marriage is an institution. Marriage is the result of love. Love is blind. Therefore, marriage is an institution for the blind.

Lucille Goodyear

1570. "My husband has only one fault. He can't seem to do anything right."

1571. If you have trouble telling the sexes apart now that both are wearing pants and long hair, just remember the one listening is the man.

1572. Inflation is what turns a nest egg into chicken feed.

1573. "As I have forgotten my notes this morning," the minister began his sermon, "I will rely on the Lord for guidance. But tonight I will come better prepared."

1574. An equal right to one's opinion carries with it an equal chance of being wrong.

1575. Blessed is the man who, having nothing to say, abstains from giving wordy evidence of that fact.

George Eliot

1576. Oliver Wendell Holmes once attended a meeting at which he was the shortest man present. A friend quipped: "Dr. Holmes, I should think you'd feel rather small among us fellows." And Holmes replied, "I do, I feel like a dime among a lot of pennies."

1577. A husband, mulling over his bills, exclaimed: "I'd give a thousand dollars to anyone who would do my worrying for me!" "You're on," answered his wife, "where's the thousand?" Replied the husband, "That's your first worry."

1578. A diplomat is a man who says you have an open mind when what he actually means is you have a hole in your head.

1579. Definition of a reformer: Someone who wants his conscience to be your guide.

1580. We've always had adult education—it's called *parenthood*.

1581. When I was a boy, my father was boss. Now I'm a man and my son is the boss. When does it get to be my turn?

Sam Levenson

1582. A Sunday school teacher asked her class to give a definition of faith. One little boy spoke right up and said: "Faith is believing something you know isn't true."

1583. I frequently quote myself. It adds spice and flavor to the conversation.

George Bernard Shaw

1584. Dog spelled backwards is still man's best friend.

1585. A diplomat is anyone who thinks twice before saying nothing.

1586. Social tact is making your guests feel at home even though you wish they were.

1587. A person gets married due to lack of judgment, divorced due to lack of patience, and remarried due to lack of money.

1588. A shiny sports car came roaring up and stopped alongside the porch of a village store where an old man was rocking in his chair. The social wildcat behind the wheel asked: "Hey, grandpa, how long has this burg been dead?" The old gentleman looked out over the top of his eyeglasses and calmly replied: "Not long, I reckon. You're the first buzzard I've seen."

1589. Junk is something you keep for years, and then throw away a week before you need it.

1590. What a world! By the time you're important enough to take two hours for lunch, the doctor limits you to a glass of milk.

1591. Today's mighty oak is yesterday's little nut that held its ground.

1592. A do-it-yourself catalog firm received this letter from a customer: "I built a bird house according to your stupid plans. Not only is it too big, but it keeps blowing out of the tree." The letter was signed, "Unhappy." The firm replied: "Dear Unhappy: Sorry! We accidentally sent you a sailboat blueprint. If you think you're unhappy, you ought to see the guy who tried to sail his leaky birdhouse in a Chicago Yacht Club race."

1593. Definition of existentialism: I and thou, here and now, Wow!

1594. A wonder drug is a medicine that makes you wonder whether you can afford to get sick.

1595. As a baby, Moses was found along the Nile by bank examiners; the banks showed a "prophet" that year.

1596. The cost of any auto repair is equal to the sum of the parts, your worst fears, and double the mechanic's estimate.

1597. Patience is the ability to count down before blasting off.

1598. When a husband bothers to open the door and help his wife into the car, he probably has just acquired one or the other.

1599. Maybe a dog is man's best friend because he wags his tail instead of his tongue.

1600. The only one who should put faith in a rabbit's foot is a rabbit.

1601. There is no wholly satisfactory substitute for brains, but silence does pretty well.

1602. A barber was eager to extend his Christian witness. While sharpening his razor on a razor strap he blurted out to his customer, "Sir, are you prepared to die?"

1603. Homework gives a youngster something to do while watching TV.

1604. Before credit cards we always knew exactly how much we were broke.

1605. The recipe for a good speech includes some shortening.

Gene Yasenak

1606. The biggest job politicians face is getting money from taxpayers without disturbing the voters.

1607. Subtlety is the art of saying what you think and getting out of range before it's understood.

F. G. Kernan

1608. Ad in newspaper: "For sale. Complete set of encyclopedias. Never used. Wife knows everything."

1609. A bargain is something you can't use at a price you can't resist.

1610. The magician who saws a woman in two is not nearly as marvelous as the husband who keeps one from flying to pieces.

1611. Wife to husband: "How was your speech at the dinner last night?" Husband to wife: "Well, when I sat down the master of ceremonies said it was the best thing I ever did."

1612. There is only one thing in the world that is worse than being talked about, and that is not being talked about.

1613. Behold the turtle. He makes progress only when he sticks out his neck.

1614. "Your sermons are so helpful. They're like water to a drowning man."

1615. If at first you don't succeed, so much for sky-diving.

1616. Some people play golf religiously—every Sunday.

1617. A classic is a book which people praise and don't read.

Mark Twain

1618. Some of the happiest people in the world today are vegetarians studying the meat prices in a super market.

1619. Public relations is the art of not treating the public like they were relation.

1620. The longest distance between two points is an unfamiliar short cut.

Gene Yasenak

1621. Hubby went out with the boys one evening and before he realized it, the morning of the next day had dawned. He hesitated to go home having been out all night. Suddenly he hit upon a great idea. He telephoned his wife and when she answered, he shouted: "Don't pay the ransom, honey. I escaped!"

1622. There is a story going around among missionaries, of the cannibal who complains that since the ecumenical movement has been underway, all missionaries taste alike.

1623. He who sleeps late on Sunday morning is sack religious.

1624. A genealogist is one who traces back your family as far as your money will go.

1625. Some people are like a wheelbarrow—useful only when pushed, and too easily upset.

1626. The woman called to the stand was exceedingly handsome but no longer young. The judge gallantly instructed: "Let the witness state her age, after which she may be sworn to tell the truth."

1627. From Scotland comes the story of the man who

was known in his congregation as being opposed to all foreign missions. When the offering plate was passed for a special missionary offering, he sat rigidly in the pew, his face set like a flint and gave nothing. On one such occasion the usher whispered to him: "Man, don't just sit there. Take something out—it's for the heathen!"

1628. A Presbyterian and a Catholic chaplain had served together in World War I and had become close friends. When they parted at the close of the war, the Presbyterian chaplain said: "Well, good-bye dear friend. We've had many profitable times together—some joyful and some sorrowful—but all meaningful. After all," he added, "both of us wish to serve the Master—you in your way and I in His."

1629. We have been given two ears and one tongue, so we ought to listen twice as much as we talk.

1630. A modern fable relates that a hen and a hog were traveling together. They passed a church that displayed the sermon subject for the coming Sunday: "How Can We Help The Poor?" After a moment's reflection the hen ventured: "I know what we can do! We can give them a ham and egg breakfast." The hog promptly replied: "You can say that because for you that's just a contribution, but for me it's total commitment."

1631. If you believe President Nixon knew nothing about Watergate, I invite you to see me when this meeting is over. I have some lovely swamp land in Florida I'd like to sell you.

Art Buchwald

1632. Today there is some good news and some bad news. The bad: we don't know where we're going. The good: we're traveling at record speeds.

1633. None preaches better than the ant and she says nothing.

Benjamin Franklin

1634. Tact: the studied ability to shut your mouth before somebody else wants to.

F. G. Kernan

1635. Blessed are those who expect nothing because they shall not be disappointed.

Alexander Pope

SOURCE LIST

1. *Church Herald*, Feb. 20, 1970, p. 2.
3. *Vital Christianity*, July 28, 1974, p. 1.
4. *Religion in Life*, Summer, 1970, p. 171.
5. *Vital Christianity*, Dec. 10, 1972, p. 18.
7. *The Mennonite*, Oct. 8, 1974, p. 579.
9. *Church Herald*, Dec. 15, 1972, p. 7.
10. *American Issue*, Mar.-Apr., 1975, p. 1.
12. *Presbyterian Journal*, Oct. 23, 1974, p. 11.
13. *Wesleyan Advocate*, Mar. 6, 1972, p. 3.
16. *The Link*, Sept., 1974, p. 59.
17. *American Opinion*, Jan., 1971, p. 75.
19. *The Link*, Apr., 1970, p. 59.
22. *The Link*, Dec., 1974, p. 46.
24. *Christian Reader*, Feb.-Mar., 1974, p. 44.
27. *Christian Reader*, Apr.-May, 1971, p. 29.
28. *War Cry*, Apr. 10, 1971, p. 8.
29. *Presbyterian Journal*, Jan. 22, 1975, p. 9.
30. *Alliance Witness*, Jan. 1, 1975, p. 7.
34. *War Cry*, Jan. 4, 1969, p. 7.
35. *Wesleyan Advocate*, Sept. 30, 1974, p. 5.
36. *The Mennonite*, Dec. 17, 1974, p. 749.
37. *Presbyterian Journal*, June 12, 1974, p. 13.
38. *Religion in Life*, Autumn, 1971, p. 376.
39. *The Congregationalist*, Dec. 1970, p. 5.
44. *Herald of Holiness*, Apr. 11, 1973, p. 16.
45. *The Link*, Oct., 1971, p. 58.
46. *The Messenger*, Feb. 15, 1972, front cover.
49. *The Banner*, July 31, 1970, p. 19.
51. *Christian Herald*, Apr., 1971, p. 29.
52. *Pentecostal Evangel*, Nov. 12, 1972, p. 4.
53. *War Cry*, Dec. 25, 1971, p. 3.
54. *Herald of Holiness*, Dec. 8, 1971, p. 15.
55. *War Cry*, Jan. 8, 1972, p. 6.
56. *Presbyterian Journal*, Sept. 1, 1971, p. 6.
57. *Presbyterian Journal*, Apr. 11, 1973, p. 13.
58. *The Banner*, Jan. 22, 1971, p. 9.
60. *Pentecostal Evangel*, Dec. 8, 1974, p. 2.
64. *Herald of Holiness*, Dec. 4, 1974, p. 18.
66. *Presbyterian Journal*, Oct. 16, 1974, p. 10.
67. *Christianity Today*, Apr. 11, 1969, p. 4.
68. *Herald of Holiness*, Dec. 4, 1974, p. 13.
69. *Pentecostal Evangel*, Dec. 8, 1974, p. 2.
70. *Presbyterian Journal*, Jan. 1, 1975, p. 8.
71. *Vital Christianity*, Nov. 16, 1969, p. 8.
73. *Herald of Holiness*, May 22, 1974, p. 15.
74. *Pentecostal Evangel*, Dec. 31, 1972, p. 12.
75. *Pentecostal Evangel*, July 18, 1971, p. 23.
76. *Baptist Bulletin*, Mar., 1972, p. 19.
78. *Presbyterian Journal*, Apr. 19, 1972, p. 17.
79. *The Link*, Mar., 1971, p. 37.
82. *The Link*, Dec., 1972, p. 63.
83. *American Opinion*, June, 1973, p. 77.
84. *Commonweal*, Nov. 6, 1970, p. 149.
85. *American Opinion*, Sept., 1971, p. 73.
86. *Vital Christianity*, Jan. 9, 1972. p. 4.
87. *The Link*, Sept., 1970, p. 58.
88. *Christian Herald*, Feb., 1971, p. 47.
90. *These Times*, May, 1971, p. 33.
91. *Lutheran Standard*, Dec. 8, 1970, p. 12.
93. *Herald of Holiness*, May 13, 1970, p. 11.
95. *Lutheran Standard*, June 5, 1973, p. 5.
101. *Presbyterian Journal*, Dec. 6, 1972, p. 13.
102. *American Opinion*, Dec., 1971, p. 64.
105. *Presbyterian Journal*, May 12, 1971, p. 8.
111. *Christian Home*, Sept., 1974, p. 9.
112. *War Cry*, Sept. 22, 1973, p. 3.
114. *The Link*, Dec., 1974, p. 54.
115. *Wesleyan Advocate*, Feb. 3, 1975, p. 1.
117. *Wesleyan Advocate*, May 28, 1973, p. 9.
118. *American Opinion*, Oct., 1970, p. 73.
119. *The Link*, Feb., 1974, p. 64.
124. *American Opinion*, Mar., 1972, p. 71.
125. *Herald of Holiness*, Apr. 10, 1974, p. 7.
126. *The Messenger*, Jan., 1974, p. 12.
127. *War Cry*, Jan. 27, 1973, p. 5.
128. *Christian Herald*, Nov., 1970, p. 25.
129. *The Christian*, Jan. 19, 1969, p. 5.
130. *Christian Standard*, Feb. 14, 1970, p. 5.
131. *The Link*, Apr., 1971, p. 58.
132. *The Banner*, Dec. 18, 1970, p. 9.
133. *The Link*, Sept., 1971, p. 13.
134. *Christianity Today*, July 19, 1968, p. 3.
135. *The Banner*, Apr. 17, 1970, p. 9.
137. *Episcopalian*, June, 1971, p. 29.
138. *Presbyterian Journal*, Jan. 22, 1975, p. 7.
139. *Christian Standard*, Oct. 17, 1971, p. 8.
140. *Presbyterian Journal*, Dec. 30, 1970, p. 12.
141. *These Times*, Apr., 1971, p. 33.
143. *The Pulpit*, Mar., 1969, p. 47.
146. *Pulpit Digest*, Dec., 1968, p. 30.
148. *War Cry*, Jan. 4, 1969, p. 7.
149. *Lutheran Witness*, July, 1972, p. 8.
150. *American Ecclesiastical Review*, Mar., 1970, p. 147.
153. *Presbyterian Journal*, Apr. 10, 1968, p. 10.
159. *The Link*, Feb., 1972, p. 59.
162. *Vital Christianity*, Oct. 19, 1969, p. 8.
163. *Pastoral Psychology*, May, 1971, p. 51.
165. *Pentecostal Evangel*, May 11, 1969, p. 9.
168. *Wesleyan Advocate*, Sept. 16, 1974, p. 9.
169. *Vital Christianity*, Apr. 15, 1973, p. 1.
170. *Christian Reader*, Dec.-Jan., 1971-2, p. 5.
171. *Christian Reader*, Dec.-Jan., 1971-72, p. 7.
172. *Christianity Today*, Apr. 27, 1973, p. 12.
173. *Church Herald*, June 28, 1974, p. 17.
175. *His*, June, 1973, p. 33.

176. *U.S. Catholic*, Aug., 1970, p. 39.
178. *Herald of Holiness*, Feb. 18, 1970, p. 10.
183. *The Link*, Oct., 1971, p. 58.
184. *Vital Christianity*, Nov. 14, 1971, p. 14.
185. *Herald of Holiness*, July 3, 1974, p. 12.
186. *The Link*, Feb., 1972, p. 59.
187. *Theology Today*, Oct., 1971, p. 295.
188. *Christian Reader*, Oct.-Nov., 1970, p. 27.
190. *Vital Christianity*, May 30, 1971, p. 5.
191. *Herald of Holiness*, Apr. 11, 1973, p. 13.
192. *The Mennonite*, Feb. 20, 1973 p. 115.
193. *Pentecostal Evangel*, June 7, 1970, p. 10.
195. *Herald of Holiness*, May 8, 1974, p. 18.
196. *Presbyterian Journal*, Apr. 17, 1974, p. 7.
197. *Wesleyan Advocate*, Feb. 18, 1974, p. 7.
198. *Eternity*, May, 1974, p. 48.
199. *Presbyterian Journal*, June 13, 1973, p. 13.
200. *Good News Broadcaster*, June, 1970, p. 11.
201. *The Banner*, July 31, 1970, p. 19.
204. *Lutheran Standard*, July 3, 1973, p. 15.
205. *Christian Herald*, Apr., 1973, p. 22.
206. *Christian Herald*, Feb., 1968, p. 23.
207. *The Pulpit*, Feb., 1969, p. 23.
209. *Vital Christianity*, Apr. 28, 1974, p. 4.
210. *Sound of the Trumpet*, Feb., 1975, p. 1.
211. *The Banner*, July 26, 1974, p. 8.
214. *Herald of Holiness*, Aug. 16, 1972, p. 5.
216. *The Messenger*, Dec., 1972, p. 36.
218. *Presbyterian Journal*, Nov. 10, 1971, p. 13.
219. *Alliance Witness*, Nov. 20, 1974, p. 3.
220. *Vital Christianity*, Feb. 8, 1970, p. 6.
221. *America*, Aug. 19, 1972, p. 94.
222. *Herald of Holiness*, Aug. 6, 1969, p. 3.
223. *Christian Standard*, Jan. 17, 1971, p. 9.
224. *The Link*, Sept., 1970, p. 46.
225. *Presbyterian Journal*, Nov. 13, 1968, p. 12.
228. *Presbyterian Journal*, Oct. 30, 1968, p. 7.
231. *Christianity Today*, June 19, 1970, p. 14.
232. *Herald of Holiness*, Sept. 11, 1974, p. 19.
237. *Good News Broadcaster*, Mar., 1972, p. 5.
238. *War Cry*, Apr. 8, 1972, p. 3.
241. *The Lutheran*, Sept. 6, 1972, p. 11.
242. *Presbyterian Journal*, Dec. 6, 1972, p. 13.
243. *War Cry*, Dec. 23, 1972, p. 13.
244. *Lutheran Witness*, Dec. 15, 1974, p. 4.
245. *Pentecostal Evangel*, Dec. 6, 1970, p. 12.
246. *Christian Century*, Dec. 25, 1974, p. 1214.
247. *The Congregationalist*, Dec., 1974, p. 3.
248. *American Opinion*, Dec., 1973, p. 29.
249. *Presbyterian Life*, Dec. 1, 1969, p. 20.
250. *American Opinion*, Dec., 1973, p. 75.
251. *Christianity Today*, Dec. 22, 1972, p. 5.
252. *Eternity*, Apr., 1970, p. 51.
253. *Presbyterian Journal*, Feb. 9, 1972, p. 11.
254. *Today's Education*, Mar., 1972, p. 29.
255. *Presbyterian Journal*, Feb. 9, 1972, p. 9.
256. *Herald of Holiness*, July 21, 1971, p. 9.
258. *Church Herald*, May 28, 1971, p. 7.
260. *The Mennonite*, Sept. 14, 1971, p. 538.
263. *The Pulpit*, May, 1969, p. 3.
264. *The Banner*, Jan. 1, 1971, p. 12.
265. *Theology Today*, Jan., 1975, p. 306.
272. *The Lutheran*, Nov. 20, 1974, p. 14.
275. *Commonweal*, Oct. 17, 1969, p. 76.

276. *United Evangelical Action*, Fall, 1969, p. 22.
277. *Christianity Today*, July 6, 1973, p. 39.
280. *War Cry*, Aug. 24, 1974, p. 3.
282. *Episcopalian*, Aug., 1971, p. 12.
284. *Presbyterian Journal*, Aug. 29, 1973, p. 7.
286. *The Banner*, Feb. 28, 1975, p. 13.
288. *War Cry*, Aug. 24, 1974, p. 3.
293. *The Mennonite*, Dec. 3, 1975, p. 718.
294. *Religious Education*, May-June, 1974, p. 84.
295. *Presbyterian Journal*, July 3, 1974, p. 13.
296. *Presbyterian Journal*, July 31, 1974, p. 12.
297. *Vital Christianity*, Sept. 17, 1972, p. 13.
300. *Pentecostal Evangel*, Mar. 12, 1972, p. 3.
302. *The Banner*, Oct. 11, 1974, p. 7.
303. *The Congregationalist*, Oct., 1974, p. 19.
304. *Christian Standard*, Sept. 5, 1971, p. 16.
305. *Herald of Holiness*, Oct. 7, 1970, p. 8.
306. *Jewish Spectator*, Nov., 1970, p. 12.
307. *Presbyterian Journal*, Apr. 18, 1973, p. 9.
308. *Church Herald*, July 28, 1972, p. 10.
311. *American Opinion*, Dec., 1973, p. 75.
312. *Presbyterian Journal*, June 21, 1967, p. 8.
313. *Herald of Holiness*, Dec. 20, 1972, p. 14.
316. *American Opinion*, Apr., 1974, p. 77.
317. *Episcopalian*, June, 1969, p. 14.
318. *Chelsea Journal*, Jan.-Feb., 1975, p. 3.
321. *Technology Review*, Mar.-Apr., 1974, p. 27.
322. *Presbyterian Journal*, Feb. 27, 1974, p. 13.
323. *Lutheran Standard*, Feb. 16, 1971, p. 7.
324. *Eternity*, Nov., 1972, p. 23.
326. *American Opinion*, July-Aug., 1974, p. 19.
327. *American Opinion*, Nov., 1973, p. 80.
328. *Presbyterian Journal*, Nov. 26, 1969, p. 11.
330. *Christianity Today*, Nov. 7, 1969, p. 31.
331. *Christian Standard*, Nov. 15, 1970, p. 10.
333. *Presbyterian Journal*, Feb. 28, 1973, p. 8.
334. *American Opinion*, Oct., 1972, p. 91.
335. *American Opinion*, Nov., 1971, p. 48.
337. *Presbyterian Journal*, Oct. 6, 1971, p. 13.
339. *Eternity*, Dec., 1970, p. 17.
342. *Presbyterian Journal*, Aug. 11, 1971, p. 13.
346. *Presbyterian Journal*, Feb. 9, 1972, p. 11.
348. *American Opinion*, June, 1973, p. 77.
349. *The Banner*, July 28, 1972, p. 18.
351. *Christianity Today*, Apr. 12, 1974, p. 58.
353. *The Lutheran*, Aug. 14, 1974, p. 14.
354. *Presbyterian Journal*, June 12, 1974, p. 11.
356. *Pentecostal Evangel*, Dec. 8, 1974, p. 16.
357. *Vital Christianity*, Aug., 1974, p. 2.
360. *Vital Christianity*, June 14, 1970, p. 13.
361. *Presbyterian Journal*, June 2, 1971, p. 22.
362. *Pentecostal Evangel*, Mar. 24, 1974, p. 6.
365. *Wesleyan Advocate*, Dec. 11, 1972, p. 3.
366. *Vital Christianity*, Oct. 29, 1972, p. 3.
367. *Good News Broadcaster*, Jan., 1974, p. 12.
368. *His*, Feb. 1971, p. 27.
371. *The Link*, Jan., 1971, p. 51.
373. *War Cry*, Oct. 28, 1972, p. 5.
374. *The Banner*, Nov. 5, 1965, p. 9.
375. *Psychology Today*, July, 1974, p. 57.
376. *Center Magazine*, Sept., 1973, p. 5.
379. *Herald of Holiness*, Mar. 5, 1969, p. 10.
380. *The Banner*, Mar. 21, 1969, p. 2.
383. *The Pulpit*, Mar., 1969, p. 20.

384. *Herald of Holiness*, Oct. 15, 1969, p. 11.
387. *American Opinion*, Sept., 1971, p. 73.
388. *Vital Christianity*, Nov. 29, 1970, p. 3.
389. *His*, Dec., 1970, p. 4.
390. *American Scholar*, Winter, 1971, p. 55.
392. *The Messenger*, Oct. 15, 1971, p. 22.
394. *American Opinion*, Sept., 1971, p. 73.
396. *Christianity Today*, Dec. 19, 1969, p. 4.
397. *American Opinion*, May, 1973, p. 16.
398. *American Opinion*, Apr., 1973, p. 75.
399. *Presbyterian Journal*, Sept. 16, 1970, p. 11.
403. *American Opinion*, Dec., 1971, p. 64.
404. *Together*, Nov., 1967, p. 38.
405. *The Link*, July, 1971, p. 49.
406. *Pentecostal Evangel*, July 29, 1973, p. 2.
409. *Commonweal*, Sept. 20, 1974, p. 499.
411. *Catholic World*, Dec. 1969, p. 115.
412. *Church Herald*, Dec. 31, 1971, p. 10.
414. *Pentecostal Evangel*, June 30, 1974, p. 21.
415. *Lighted Pathway*, Jan. 1972, p. 14.
417. *Herald of Holiness*, Oct. 23, 1974, p. 17.
418. *American Scholar*, Autumn, 1974, p. 556.
421. *Christian Ministry*, Nov., 1974, p. 24.
422. *Critic*, Sept.-Oct., 1973, p. 28.
423. *Presbyterian Journal*, Mar. 24, 1971, p. 11.
424. *Christianity Today*, Mar. 31, 1972, p. 21.
425. *Christian Ministry*, Nov., 1974, p. 24.
428. *Presbyterian Journal*, Jan. 20, 1971, p. 12.
429. *His*, Jan., 1974, p. 17.
433. *American Opinion*, Apr., 1974, p. 77.
434. *Encounter*, Summer, 1974, p. 267.
435. *Christian Standard*, Jan. 26, 1975, p. 12.
436. *Today's Education*, Nov.-Dec. 1974, p. 17.
437. *The Link*, Dec., 1972, p. 53.
439. *The Link*, Feb., 1972, p. 59.
441. *Christian Standard*, Nov. 15, 1970, p. 10.
442. *Lutheran Standard*, Feb. 16, 1971, p. 6.
443. *The Banner*, June 7, 1974, p. 3.
446. *Herald of Holiness*, Feb. 16, 1972, p. 5.
447. *Moody Monthly*, Feb. 1975, p. 3.
448. *American Opinion*, Nov., 1970, p. 72.
449. *The Banner*, July 10, 1970, p. 12.
451. *American Opinion*, Apr., 1974, p. 77.
452. *United Evangelical Action*, Summer, 1974, p. 27.
453. *Christianity Today*, Apr. 12, 1974, p. 7.
457. *American Opinion*, Dec., 1970, p. 20.
458. *American Opinion*, Sept., 1974, p. 30.
460. *Christianity Today*, Sept. 26, 1969, p. 36.
462. *Applied Christianity*, Aug., 1974, p. 37.
464. *Christianity Today*, Dec. 8, 1972, p. 53.
465. *Church Herald*, Feb. 21, 1975, p. 11.
466. *Applied Christianity*, July, 1974, p. 7.
467. *American Opinion*, Dec., 1973, p. 76.
468. *Daedalus*, Fall, 1974, p. 111.
469. *Daedalus*, Fall, 1974, p. 41.
470. *Church Herald*, Dec. 18, 1970, p. 5.
471. *American Opinion*, Mar., 1972, p. 71.
472. *American Opinion*, June, 1971, p. 71.
476. *War Cry*, Oct. 9, 1971, p. 7.
477. *Pentecostal Evangel*, Sept. 15, 1974, p. 2.
481. *Vital Christianity*, May 30, 1971, p. 3.
482. *The Link*, Nov., 1971, p. 39.
483. *Presbyterian Journal*, Feb. 9, 1972, p. 13.
484. *The Link*, Oct., 1971, p. 62.
485. *Presbyterian Journal*, June 12, 1974, p. 9.
486. *Herald of Holiness*, Feb. 16, 1972, p.5.
487. *Christian Reader*, Feb.-Mar., 1974, p. 36.
490. *Vital Christianity*, Feb. 16, 1975, p. 10.
491. *Herald of Holiness*, Nov. 19, 1969, p. 10.
492. *Herald of Holiness*, Jan. 19, 1966, p. 11.
493. *The Banner*, Dec. 25, 1970, p. 15.
496. *The Christian*, Nov. 3, 1968, p. 28.
497. *Pentecostal Evangel*, Sept. 8, 1974, p. 2.
500. *The Link*, Feb., 1973, p. 63.
505. *Lutheran Standard*, Dec. 8, 1970, p. 11.
506. *Herald of Holiness*, Nov. 4, 1970, p. 7.
507. *These Times*, Dec., 1970, p. 15.
508. *The Mennonite*, Oct. 17, 1972, p. 612.
510. *Christianity Today*, Nov. 8, 1974, p. 16.
511. *Religious Education*, Mar.-Apr., 1974, p. 248.
512. *Eternity*, Aug., 1971, p. 29.
513. *The Link*, Mar., 1971, p. 37.
518. *Lighted Pathway*, July, 1970, p. 11.
519. *Christian Reader*, Nov.-Dec., 1974, p. 7.
521. *Herald of Holiness*, July 31, 1974, p. 18.
522. *Presbyterian Journal*, July 24, 1974, p. 8.
523. *Herald of Holiness*, Mar. 27, 1974, p. 19.
524. *Christian Advocate*, Jan. 7, 1971, p. 8.
525. *Herald of Holiness*, May 8, 1974, p. 18.
527. *Presbyterian Journal*, Apr. 8, 1970, p. 8.
528. *American Opinion*, Jan., 1971, p. 75.
529. *The Banner*, Oct. 25, 1974, p. 15.
530. *Presbyterian Journal*, Jan. 13, 1971, p. 10.
531. *The Mennonite*, Nov. 9, 1971, p. 675.
533. *Pentecostal Evangel*, Feb. 24, 1974, p. 30.
534. *The Mennonite*, Sept. 23, 1969, p. 574.
535. *The Mennonite*, May 8, 1973, p. 301.
538. *American Opinion*, Oct., 1974, p. 31.
540. *The Link*, Jan., 1972, p. 55.
543. *Eternity*, Nov., 1974, p. 30.
544. *American Opinion*, Jan., 1974, p. 77.
545. *Herald of Holiness*, Oct. 15, 1969, p. 11.
546. *War Cry*, Apr. 19, 1969, p. 22.
547. *American Opinion*, Dec., 1972, p. 85.
551. *American Opinion*, June, 1973, p. 77.
552. *U.S. Catholic*, Sept., 1974, p. 36.
554. *American Opinion*, Dec., 1970, p. 20.
555. *American Opinion*, Nov., 1970, p. 71.
556. *Christian Century*, Feb. 19, 1975, p. 161.
557. *War Cry*, Nov. 11, 1972, p. 8.
558. *Baptist Bulletin*, Dec., 1971, p. 10.
559. *U.S. Catholic*, Mar., 1972, p. 14.
560. *Mission*, Mar., 1969, p. 51.
561. *Christian Home*, Dec., 1973, p. 4.
562. *His*, Jan., 1975, p. 32.
563. *Christian Standard*, Apr. 25, 1970, p. 15.
564. *War Cry*, Jan. 8, 1972, p. 6.
565. *Presbyterian Journal*, July 1, 1970, p. 13.
566. *His*, Feb., 1969, p. 10.
567. *American Opinion*, Mar., 1974, p. 77.
571. *American Opinion*, Mar., 1972, p. 72.
573. *The Banner*, June 30, 1972, p. 2.
575. *The Pulpit*, Mar., 1969, p. 19.
576. *Church Herald*, Apr. 17, 1970, p. 22.
578. *The Christian*, Oct. 20, 1968, p. 4.
579. *The Link*, Apr., 1970, p. 12.

580. *Vital Christianity*, June 30, 1974, p. 3.
582. *The Link*, Dec., 1974, p. 54.
583. *U.S. Catholic*, Oct., 1970, p. 38.
584. *Christian Herald*, May, 1972, p. 50.
588. *American Opinion*, Nov., 1972, p. 91.
591. *The Mennonite*, May 22, 1973, p. 330.
592. *The Link*, July, 1974, p. 23.
593. *Christianity Today*, Mar. 29, 1968, p. 15.
594. *Good News Broadcaster*, Apr., 1971, p. 26.
596. *Good News Broadcaster*, Sept., 1971, p. 25.
597. *Episcopalian*, Oct., 1972, p. 29
598. *His*, Jan., 1973, p. 1.
599. *Catholic World*, Jan., 1970, p. 159.
600. *Episcopalian*, Feb., 1971, p. 12.
601. *Jewish Frontier*, Oct., 1974, p. 24.
602. *Wesleyan Advocate*, Aug. 5, 1974, p. 7.
603. *Alliance Witness*, Oct. 9, 1974, p. 3.
604. *Church Herald*, June 28, 1974, p. 2.
611. *Pentecostal Evangel*, July 7, 1974, p. 16.
612. *Christian Standard*, Jan. 24, 1971, p. 8.
613. *Episcopalian*, July, 1971, p. 24.
615. *His*, Dec., 1973, p. 6.
616. *The Pulpit*, Apr., 1969, p. 23.
617. *Christianity Today*, Mar. 17, 1972, p. 4.
618. *Vital Christianity*, Dec. 29, 1968, p. 3.
619. *Pentecostal Evangel*, Oct. 13, 1974, p. 15.
624. *Christian Reader*, Feb.-Mar., 1972, p. 31.
625. *The Mennonite*, Jan. 8, 1974, p. 32.
627. *The Link*, Apr., 1970, p. 12.
628. *Herald of Holiness*, Sept. 26, 1973, p. 3.
630. *A.D.*, July, 1974, p. 27.
632. *Christian Standard*, Apr. 25, 1970, p. 15.
633. *War Cry*, Nov. 18, 1972, p. 7.
634. *The Banner*, July 10, 1970, p. 12.
635. *Herald of Holiness*, July 3, 1974, p. 18.
636. *Pulpit Digest*, Feb., 1969, p. 39.
640. *Herald of Holiness*, Feb. 16, 1972, p. 6.
641. *The Banner*, Oct. 8, 1971, p. 2.
642. *War Cry*, May 22, 1971, p. 24.
645. *Lutheran Witness*, Sept. 2, 1972, p. 3.
646. *Lutheran Standard*, Sept. 5, 1972, p. 35.
648. *Evangel*, Feb. 11, 1974, p. 27.
649. *Herald of Holiness*, July 3, 1974, p. 18.
650. *Herald of Holiness*, July 3, 1974, p. 18.
652. *The Link*, Feb., 1973, p. 47.
653. *Lutheran Witness*, Nov. 3, 1974, p. 6.
656. *Wesleyan Advocate*, Feb. 3, 1975, p. 9.
657. *The Link*, July, 1974, p. 23.
658. *Presbyterian Journal*, Jan. 1, 1975, p. 11.
659. *His*, Apr., 1973, p. 16.
660. *Pentecostal Evangel*, Sept. 8, 1974, p. 3.
662. *The Link*, Feb., 1970, p. 37.
663. *Wesleyan Advocate*, Feb. 21, 1972, p. 4.
664. *His*, Apr., 1973, p. 16.
666. *Presbyterian Journal*, July 3, 1974, p. 12.
669. *Presbyterian Journal*, Dec. 11, 1974, p. 7.
671. *Theology Today*, Jan., 1971, p. 382.
672. *Today's Education*, Sept., 1972, p. 64.
675. *Christian Century*, May 13, 1970, p. 597.
676. *Pentecostal Evangel*, Feb. 17, 1974, p. 31.
677. *The Banner*, June 7, 1974, p. 3.
678. *Wesleyan Advocate*, Nov. 25, 1974, p. 2.
679. *Christianity Today*, Aug. 16, 1974, p. 7.
680. *Christian Herald*, Oct., 1974, p. 14.
681. *Christian Herald*, Oct., 1974, p. 14.
682. *Christian Herald*, Oct., 1974, p. 16.
683. *The Link*, Jan., 1974, p. 14.
684. *Herald of Holiness*, Jan. 1, 1975, p. 19.
685. *Christianity Today*, Aug. 16, 1974, p. 6.
687. *Christian Reader*, Dec.-Jan., 1971-72, p. 61.
689. *Vital Christianity*, Sept. 30, 1973, p. 4.
690. *Pentecostal Evangel*, Sept. 22, 1974, p. 2.
691. *His*, Jan., 1973, p. 3.
692. *Herald of Holiness*, June 7, 1972, p. 13.
693. *Christian Herald*, May, 1973, p. 7.
694. *The Link*, July, 1971, p. 49.
695. *The Link*, May, 1971, p. 43.
696. *Christian Life*, Jan., 1974, p. 70.
697. *Presbyterian Journal*, July 24, 1974, p. 13.
698. *Midnight Call*, Apr., 1974, p. 4.
700. *Christian Reader*, Feb.-Mar., 1974, p. 36.
701. *Herald of Holiness*, July 21, 1971, p. 9.
702. *Vital Christianity*, June 30, 1974, p. 1.
703. *Christianity Today*, July 6, 1973, p. 39.
704. *Vital Christianity*, June 30, 1974, p. 2.
707. *Vital Christianity*, Mar. 3, 1974, p. 3.
708. *The Link*, Dec., 1972, p. 63.
713. *Today's Education*, Mar.-Apr., 1974, p. 26.
714. *American Opinion*, Nov., 1970, p. 71.
715. *Vital Christianity*, Oct. 5, 1969, p. 14.
716. *American Opinion*, June, 1973, p. 77.
717. *Church Herald*, Mar. 31, 1972, p. 5.
719. *Herald of Holiness*, Jan. 18, 1974, p. 8.
720. *American Opinion*, Oct., 1970, p. 73.
723. *These Times*, Mar., 1970, p. 34.
724. *The Mennonite*, Nov. 9, 1971, p. 675.
725. *American Opinion*, Jan., 1972, p. 77.
730. *Daedalus*, Fall, 1974, p. 300.
731. *The Link*, July, 1970, p. 66.
732. *U.S. Catholic*, Jan., 1975, p. 22.
733. *American Opinion*, Jan., 1975, p. 33.
734. *American Opinion*, Mar., 1973, p. 95.
735. *Moody Monthly*, Jan., 1975, p. 29.
736. *The Link*, Oct., 1974, p. 61.
737. *The Link*, Apr., 1970, p. 12.
739. *Moody Monthly*, July-Aug., 1970, p. 50.
741. *Soundings*, Spring, 1973, p. 45.
743. *Christian Ministry*, July, 1972, p. 40.
745. *The Mennonite*, Oct. 9, 1973, p. 572.
747. *Presbyterian Journal*, Jan. 13, 1971, p. 10.
748. *Vital Christianity*, May 30, 1971, p. 3.
749. *Evangel*, Dec. 9, 1974, p. 9.
750. *Presbyterian Journal*, Mar. 3, 1971, p. 9.
753. *The Messenger*, Dec. 3, 1970, p. 32.
755. *Presbyterian Journal*, Jan. 6, 1971, p. 1.
757. *Presbyterian Journal*, Jan. 1, 1975, p. 8.
759. *Pentecostal Evangel*, Sept. 8, 1974, p. 3.
760. *Moody Monthly*, Jan., 1975, p. 65.
761. *Pentecostal Evangel*, Dec. 31, 1972, p. 11.
762. *Christianity Today*, Mar. 29, 1974, p. 30.
763. *The Link*, June, 1971, p. 41.
765. *Jewish Spectator*, Oct., 1970, p. 8.
767. *The Christian*, Mar. 16, 1969, p. 14.
768. *The Link*, Oct., 1971, p. 62.
770. *The Link*, Feb., 1972, p. 59.
771. *The Link*, Apr., 1973, p. 62.
773. *American Opinion*, Jan., 1975, p. 33.
774. *American Opinion*, Oct., 1974, p. 31.

775. *Vital Christianity*, Aug. 22, 1971, p. 5.
778. *The Congregationalist*, Feb., 1974, p. 7.
780. *The Pulpit*, Feb., 1969, p. 25.
781. *The Link*, Jan., 1971, p. 33.
782. *American Opinion*, Oct., 1970, p. 73.
783. *American Opinion*, Jan., 1971, p. 75.
784. *American Opinion*, Jan., 1972, p. 77.
785. *American Opinion*, Nov., 1972, p. 91.
786. *Vital Christianity*, Aug. 25, 1974, p. 17.
790. *Vital Christianity*, Feb. 21, 1971, p. 5.
791. *America*, Apr. 21, 1973, p. 362.
795. *Presbyterian Journal*, Mar. 8, 1972, p. 13.
796. *Herald of Holiness*, Mar. 26, 1969, p. 10.
798. *Lutheran Standard*, May 2, 1972, p. 11.
799. *Christian Standard*, Feb. 27, 1972, p. 13.
800. *These Times*, Dec., 1970, p. 5.
801. *His*, Oct., 1971, p. 32.
802. *Wesleyan Advocate*, Aug. 5, 1974, p. 7.
803. *Herald of Holiness*, May 8, 1974, p. 18.
805. *Christian Herald*, Jan., 1971, p. 39.
806. *The Link*, Nov., 1972, p. 47.
807. *These Times*, May, 1971, p. 5.
810. *The Link*, Mar., 1971, p. 37.
811. *American Scholar*, Autumn, 1974, p. 553.
813. *The Link*, Sept., 1970, p. 58.
815. *Christian Reader*, Apr.-May, 1971, p. 29.
816. *A.D.*, Oct., 1974, p. 45.
817. *Vital Christianity*, May 2, 1971, p. 3.
822. *Covenant Companion*, Mar. 1, 1970, p. 32.
823. *The Christian*, Feb. 4, 1968, p. 10.
824. *Religious Humanism*, Summer, 1969, p. 112
829. *Annals*, Jan., 1973, p. 86.
830. *Christian Home*, Sept., 1971, p. 14.
831. *Pentecostal Evangel*, Feb. 25, 1974, p. 23.
832. *Cross Currents*, Summer-Fall, 1972, p. 231.
834. *Lutheran Standard*, May 2, 1972, p. 11.
835. *Religious Humanism*, Autumn, 1971, p. 167
836. *Herald of Holiness*, Aug. 4, 1971, p. 14.
838. *The Messenger*, Sept. 1, 1971, p. 21.
839. *Christian Herald*, Jan., 1971, p. 39.
840. *Moody Monthly*, Jan., 1975, p. 47.
842. *Eternity*, Sept., 1968, p. 16.
847. *Lutheran Standard*, Jan. 19, 1971, p. 7.
848. *Critic*, Sept.-Oct., 1969, p. 17.
849. *Lutheran Witness*, Mar. 17, 1974, p. 5.
850. *American Opinion*, Nov., 1972, p. 91.
852. *The Link*, Dec., 1970, p. 58.
856. *Presbyterian Journal*, May 23, 1973, p. 8.
862. *Good News Broadcaster*, Apr., 1971, p. 26.
863. *The Pulpit*, Apr., 1969, p. 23.
866. *American Opinion*, July-Aug., 1974, p. 18.
867. *Christianity Today*, Feb. 1, 1974, p. 4.
868. *Christian Reader*, Dec.-Jan., 1971-72, p. 58.
869. *Church Advocate*, Dec., 1970, p. 21.
870. *The Banner*, Nov. 8, 1974, p. 3.
873. *Church Herald*, June 28, 1974, p. 16.
874. *The Mennonite*, June 25, 1974, p. 423.
875. *Vital Christianity*, July 12, 1970, p. 5.
876. *Church Herald*, Apr. 14, 1972, p. 7.
877. *Pentecostal Evangel*, June 11, 1972, p. 23.
881. *War Cry*, Aug. 10, 1968, p. 2.
883. *Presbyterian Journal*, Jan. 9, 1974, p. 13.
885. *Herald of Holiness*, Oct. 13, 1971, p. 17.
886. *The Link*, Dec., 1972, p. 63.

888. *Christian Home*, Sept., 1971, p. 12.
890. *U.S. Catholic*, Mar., 1970, p. 35.
893. *The Link*, Sept., 1971, p. 66.
896. *Good News Broadcaster*, Oct., 1971, p. 31.
897. *Moody Monthly*, June, 1974, p. 29.
901. *Christian Century*, Feb. 19, 1975, p. 161.
902. *Christian Life*, Jan., 1974, p. 69.
903. *Christian Life*, Mar., 1974, p. 38.
909. *Herald of Holiness*, Jan. 20, 1971, p. 9.
910. *Lutheran Witness*, Nov., 1969, p. 12.
911. *Pulpit Digest*, Feb., 1969, p. 39.
912. *Wesleyan Advocate*, Dec. 9, 1974, p. 5.
915. *U.S. Catholic*, Apr., 1970, p. 33.
917. *Christianity Today*, Dec. 8, 1972, p. 54.
920. *Church Herald*, May, 1974, p. 9.
921. *Change*, May, 1973, p. 27.
923. *Commentary*, June, 1974, p. 62.
925. *Wesleyan Advocate*, July 8, 1974, p. 5.
926. *The Link*, Dec., 1971, p. 31.
927. *Pentecostal Evangel*, Sept. 29, 1974, p. 31.
928. *Wesleyan Advocate*, May 28, 1973, p. 9.
929. *American Opinion*, Dec., 1970, p. 15.
932. *Pentecostal Evangel*, Mar. 17, 1974, p. 31.
933. *War Cry*, Mar. 2, 1974, p. 3.
935. *Daedalus*, Summer, 1974, p. 19.
936. *Herald of Holiness*, Apr. 10, 1974, p. 13.
937. *War Cry*, Mar. 2, 1974, p. 10.
939. *Church Herald*, Sept. 25, 1970, p. 14.
940. *America*, Jan. 30, 1971, p. 97.
941. *Lutheran Standard*, Sept. 21, 1971, p. 12.
943. *Pulpit Digest*, Feb., 1969, p. 26.
946. *The Banner*, Sept. 6, 1974, p. 11.
947. *Worldview*, May, 1972, p. 20.
948. *Herald of Holiness*, Sept. 25, 1974, p. 18.
949. *Presbyterian Journal*, Oct. 4, 1972, p. 13.
950. *Presbyterian Journal*, May 3, 1972, p. 15.
952. *The Banner*, June 6, 1969, p. 14.
953. *These Times*, Sept., 1971, p. 17.
955. *Presbyterian Journal*, Nov. 3, 1971, p. 20.
956. *Presbyterian Journal*, Jan. 26, 1972, p. 17.
957. *Theological Educator*, Apr., 1971, p. 15.
958. *Christianity Today*, Dec. 18, 1970, p. 25.
959. *Critic*, Jan.-Feb., 1973, p. 44.
961. *His*, Feb., 1975, p. 24.
968. *The Christian*, May 3, 1970, p. 15.
970. *U.S. Catholic*, Apr., 1970, p. 33.
971. *Vital Christianity*, Aug. 22, 1971, p. 13.
973. *Vital Christianity*, Sept. 16, 1973, p. 3.
974. *American Opinion*, Mar., 1974, p. 96.
975. *Good News Broadcaster*, May, 1971, p. 20.
978. *Christian Standard*, Sept. 20, 1969, p. 9.
984. *These Times*, Oct. 1, 1970, p. 33.
985. *War Cry*, Feb. 19, 1972, p. 24.
986. *War Cry*, Jan. 4, 1969, p. 7.
988. *Religious Humanism*, Winter, 1975, p. 24.
989. *Pentecostal Evangel*, Dec. 29, 1974, p. 2.
991. *American Opinion*, Nov., 1972, p. 91.
992. *Wesleyan Advocate*, July 10, 1972, p. 13.
993. *Pentecostal Evangel*, Jan. 6, 1974, p. 2.
994. *The Congregationalist*, Jan., 1974, p. 19.
996. *Pentecostal Evangel*, Dec. 29, 1974, p. 7.
997. *The Banner*, Aug. 24, 1973, p. 10.
998. *Herald of Holiness*, July 15, 1970, p. 10.
999. *The Link*, Jan., 1971, p. 51.

1001. *Episcopalian*, Oct., 1972, p. 29.
1002. *Christian Reader*, Feb.-Mar., 1973, p. 6.
1003. *Lutheran Standard*, May 2, 1972, p. 11.
1004. *American Opinion*, Oct., 1970, p. 73.
1005. *Today's Education*, Mar., 1972, p. 29.
1008. *Christian Home*, May, 1974, p. 11.
1011. *The Lutheran*, Oct. 4, 1972, p. 10.
1013. *Presbyterian Journal*, Apr. 5, 1972, p. 8.
1014. *Today's Education*, Mar., 1972, p. 53.
1015. *The Banner*, Apr. 13, 1973, p. 18.
1018. *American Opinion*, Apr., 1973, p. 76.
1020. *U.S. Catholic*, Sept., 1970. p. 11.
1024. *Christian Standard*, May 9, 1970, p. 8.
1027. *The Link*, July, 1970, p. 17.
1029. *Christian Life*, May, 1969, p. 23.
1030. *Baptist Bulletin*, June, 1970, p. 11.
1031. *Wesleyan Advocate*, Sept. 30, 1974, p. 5.
1032. *Christian Life*, Oct., 1973, p. 25.
1033. *American Opinion*, Mar., 1974, p. 94.
1034. *American Opinion*, Mar., 1974, p. 77.
1035. *American Opinion*, Oct., 1970, p. 74.
1037. *Today's Education*, Sept., 1972, p. 64.
1040. *Watchman Examiner*, June 26, 1969, p. 398.
1043. *American Opinion*, Jan., 1971, p. 76.
1044. *The Banner*, Nov. 7, 1969, p. 8.
1047. *American Opinion*, Sept., 1972, p. 35.
1048. *American Opinion*, May, 1972, p. 77.
1049. *Presbyterian Journal*, Dec. 4, 1974, p. 13.
1052. *American Opinion*, June, 1971, p. 71.
1054. *Nazarene Preacher*, Oct., 1964, p. 11.
1057. *Herald of Holiness*, Aug. 16, 1972, p. 5.
1058. *War Cry*, June 24, 1967, p. 11.
1059. *Pentecostal Evangel*, Feb. 17, 1974, p. 31.
1060. *Christianity Today*, Mar. 12, 1971, p. 25.
1061. *Today's Education*, Mar., 1972, p. 53.
1062. *His*, Jan., 1974, p. 17.
1065. *Presbyterian Journal*, Dec. 11, 1974, p. 11.
1066. *Presbyterian Journal*, Oct. 6, 1971, p. 13.
1067. *Alliance Witness*, Nov. 25, 1970, p. 8.
1071. *The Messenger*, June 4, 1970, p. 9.
1072. *Eternity*, Dec., 1970, p. 17.
1075. *Herald of Holiness*, Apr. 10, 1974, p. 13.
1076. *The Link*, Oct., 1971, p. 58.
1077. *Lutheran Standard*, May 2, 1972, p. 11.
1078. *Christian Herald*, Nov., 1970, p. 33.
1079. *The Link*, Apr., 1974, p. 63.
1080. *The Link*, Jan., 1971, p. 51.
1082. *Presbyterian Journal*, Oct. 16, 1974, p. 9.
1085. *Catholic Mind*, Jan., 1969, p. 38.
1087. *American Opinion*, Mar., 1973, p. 95.
1088. *Herald of Holiness*, July 1, 1970, p. 11.
1089. *Lighted Pathway*, Aug., 1969, p. 6.
1091. *American Scholar*, Autumn, 1974, p. 553.
1092. *Presbyterian Journal*, Nov. 3, 1971, p. 12.
1093. *Commentary*, Nov., 1974, p. 36.
1094. *American Opinion*, June, 1974, p. 77.
1095. *Christian Century*, Dec. 11, 1974, p. 1164.
1096. *American Opinion*, June, 1974, p. 77.
1097. *Presbyterian Journal*, Oct. 16, 1974, p. 10.
1098. *American Opinion*, July-Aug., 1974, p. 19.
1099. *Presbyterian Journal*, Nov. 20, 1974, p. 11.
1104. *The Link*, May, 1972, p. 63.
1105. *Applied Christianity*, Apr., 1973, p. 9.
1106. *Christian Century*, Feb. 26, 1975, p. 196.
1107. *These Times*, May, 1971, p. 5.
1108. *Presbyterian Journal*, Oct. 16, 1974, p. 10.
1109. *Christianity Today*, Mar. 12, 1971, p. 16.
1110. *Center Magazine*, Jan.-Feb., 1971, p. 17.
1111. *Herald of Holiness*, Apr. 26, 1972, p. 15.
1112. *Christian Herald*, July, 1971, p. 13.
1113. *American Opinion*, May, 1972, p. 77.
1114. *Religious Humanism*, Summer, 1970, p. 116.
1116. *American Opinion*, June, 1973, p. 39.
1117. *American Opinion*, Mar., 1974, p. 77.
1118. *Christian Century*, Apr. 15, 1970, p. 436.
1119. *Herald of Holiness*, July 15, 1970, p. 5.
1122. *Episcopalian*, Mar., 1972, p. 2.
1129. *Pentecostal Evangel*, Sept. 8, 1974, p. 3.
1130. *Presbyterian Journal*, Aug. 14, 1974, p. 10.
1131. *Christian Life*, Jan., 1974, p. 70.
1133. *Lighted Pathway*, Apr., 1970, p. 11.
1134. *Pentecostal Evangel*, Feb. 2, 1975, p. 15.
1135. *The Pulpit*, Mar., 1969, p. 47.
1137. *Moody Monthly*, June, 1974, p. 29.
1138. *Church Herald*, July 26, 1974, p. 9.
1141. *Pentecostal Evangel*, Oct. 17, 1971, p. 4.
1142. *Church Herald*, Dec. 13, 1974, p. 11.
1143. *These Times*, May, 1971, p. 33.
1145. *Eternity*, June, 1970, p. 50.
1146. *Pentecostal Evangel*, Feb. 28, 1971, p. 4.
1149. *Pentecostal Evangel*, Dec. 29, 1974, p. 8.
1150. *Christian Herald*, May, 1970, p. 13.
1152. *Christian Herald*, May, 1970, p. 13.
1153. *Christian Herald*, May, 1972, p. 55.
1154. *Pentecostal Evangel*, July 1, 1973, p. 11.
1155. *Herald of Holiness*, Feb. 26, 1975, p. 16.
1156. *Vital Christianity*, May 26, 1974, p. 4.
1157. *Church Herald*, July 14, 1972, p. 17.
1160. *Wesleyan Advocate*, May 17, 1971, p. 10.
1162. *Moody Monthly*, Feb., 1971, p. 53.
1163. *Herald of Holiness*, Nov. 6, 1974, p. 19.
1165. *Wesleyan Advocate*, Feb. 21, 1972, p. 4.
1169. *Wesleyan Advocate*, Feb. 17, 1975, p. 8.
1171. *American Opinion*, Apr., 1973, p. 75.
1172. *Church Herald*, Feb. 25, 1972, p. 11.
1173. *Presbyterian Journal*, Sept. 18, 1974, p. 10.
1174. *Presbyterian Journal*, Apr. 24, 1974, p. 9.
1176. *Wesleyan Methodist*, Dec. 14, 1970, p. 3.
1177. *Church Herald*, Dec., 1971, p. 11.
1178. *Christian Herald*, Nov., 1970, p. 33.
1180. *Church Herald*, June 28, 1974, p. 3.
1182. *Lutheran Standard*, Dec. 8, 1970, p. 12.
1183. *Church Herald*, Jan. 25, 1974, p. 8.
1185. *Christian Herald*, Nov., 1970, p. 24.
1187. *Presbyterian Journal*, Jan. 6, 1971, p. 9.
1188. *Christianity and Crisis*, Apr. 29, 1974, p. 90.
1189. *The Banner*, Mar. 21, 1969, p. 8.
1191. *Presbyterian Journal*, Jan. 6, 1971, p. 9.
1195. *Presbyterian Journal*, Sept. 13, 1972, p. 9.
1196. *These Times*, Nov., 1970, p. 23.
1197. *Presbyterian Journal*, Jan. 12, 1972, p. 13.
1199. *The Banner*, June 27, 1969, p. 9.
1200. *War Cry*, Oct. 10, 1970, p. 7.
1201. *Presbyterian Journal*, Feb. 26, 1975, p. 20.
1202. *America*, Dec. 15, 1973, p. 463.
1204. *Lutheran Standard*, Dec. 8, 1970, p. 12.

1206. *Church Herald*, Nov. 14, 1969, p. 6.
1207. *Christianity Today*, Dec. 3, 1971, p. 37.
1208. *Herald of Holiness*, Nov. 10, 1971, p. 16.
1209. *Christianity Today*, July 2, 1971, p. 20.
1210. *The Banner*, Apr. 27, 1973, p. 18.
1212. *The Banner*, Oct. 25, 1968, p. 2.
1213. *The Congregationalist*, June, 1971, p. 7.
1214. *Pastoral Psychology*, May, 1971, p. 26.
1215. *Presbyterian Life*, Jan. 1, 1971, p. 18.
1217. *Wesleyan Advocate*, Aug. 5, 1974, p. 7.
1221. *Journal of American Academy of Religion*, Mar., 1972, p. 21.
1224. *Eternity*, May, 1971, p. 15.
1225. *Pentecostal Evangel*, July 23, 1972, p. 5.
1228. *His*, Jan., 1975, p. 32.
1231. *Presbyterian Journal*, Nov. 17, 1971, p. 19.
1232. *Alliance Witness*, Jan. 6, 1974, p. 7.
1233. *Presbyterian Journal*, May 30, 1973, p. 13.
1234. *Presbyterian Journal*, May 26, 1971, p. 10.
1235. *Herald of Holiness*, Nov. 20, 1974, p. 19.
1236. *War Cry*, Apr. 18, 1970, p. 6.
1237. *Presbyterian Journal*, Mar. 29, 1972, p. 20.
1238. *The Banner*, Dec. 8, 1972, p. 11.
1239. *Wesleyan Advocate*, Nov. 11, 1974, p. 3.
1241. *Vital Christianity*, Dec. 1, 1974, p. 4.
1245. *American Scholar*, Winter, 1971, p. 55.
1247. *Pentecostal Evangel*, Aug. 26, 1974, p. 16.
1248. *Church Herald*, Feb. 21, 1975, p. 11.
1249. *Wesleyan Advocate*, July 22, 1974, p. 5.
1256. *His*, Jan., 1973, p. 3.
1257. *U.S. Catholic*, Aug., 1970, p. 39.
1261. *Wesleyan Advocate*, Sept. 16, 1974, p. 5.
1263. *These Times*, July, 1971, p. 33.
1264. *Hour of Decision*, Jan. 14, 1973.
1267. *Presbyterian Journal*, Mar. 31, 1971, p. 8.
1268. *The Link*, June, 1970, p. 7.
1269. *Wesleyan Advocate*, Jan. 10, 1972, p. 7.
1270. *Herald of Holiness*, Apr. 24, 1974, p. 17.
1272. *Christian Herald*, June, 1970, p. 11.
1273. *His*, Oct., 1974, p. 33.
1274. *Vital Christianity*, June 30, 1974, p. 1.
1275. *Herald of Holiness*, Oct. 21, 1970, p. 11.
1276. *The Mennonite*, Oct. 7, 1969, p. 595.
1277. *Presbyterian Journal*, July 3, 1974, p. 13.
1280. *Presbyterian Journal*, May 30, 1973, p. 13.
1281. *Presbyterian Journal*, Mar. 15, 1972, p. 13.
1282. *Herald of Holiness*, Oct. 29, 1969, p. 11.
1283. *Christian Standard*, Oct. 11, 1970, p. 12.
1284. *The Link*, Apr., 1970, p. 12.
1286. *His*, May, 1970, p. 2.
1287. *United Evangelical Action*, Fall, 1975, p. 27
1289. *Pentecostal Evangel*, Feb. 10, 1975, p. 19.
1293. *The Mennonite*, Mar. 21, 1972, p. 194.
1295. *Vital Christianity*, Nov. 14, 1971, p. 14.
1296. *Christian Standard*, Oct. 17, 1971, p. 8.
1297. *Vital Christianity*, Mar. 19, 1973, p. 10.
1298. *War Cry*, Aug. 10, 1968, p. 2.
1299. *Commentary*, Nov., 1974, p. 36.
1300. *Vital Christianity*, July 28, 1974, p. 1.
1301. *Christian Century*, Dec. 25, 1974, p. 1223.
1303. *Pastoral Psychology*, Dec., 1971, p. 5.
1305. *Wesleyan Advocate*, Oct. 28, 1974, p. 8.
1306. *Wesleyan Advocate*, Oct. 28, 1974, p. 8.
1307. *These Times*, Dec., 1970, p. 5.
1310. *Vital Christianity*, June 30, 1974, p. 1.
1313. *The Link*, Mar., 1974, p. 64.
1314. *Pentecostal Evangel*, Nov. 11, 1973, p. 19.
1317. *War Cry*, Sept. 25, 1971, p. 7.
1320. *Pentecostal Evangel*, Feb. 23, 1975, p. 6.
1323. *Pentecostal Evangel*, Nov. 19, 1972, p. 17.
1324. *Wesleyan Advocate*, May 17, 1971, p. 3.
1325. *American Ecclesiastical Review*, Sept., 1971, p. 51.
1329. *Presbyterian Journal*, Jan. 20, 1971, p. 13.
1332. *Vital Christianity*, Dec. 29, 1968, p. 2.
1335. *Presbyterian Journal*, Feb. 28, 1973, p. 8.
1336. *American Opinion*, July-Aug., 1974, p. 19.
1337. *American Opinion*, Dec., 1973, p. 75.
1338. *American Opinion*, Nov., 1974, p. 21.
1341. *Good News Broadcaster*, Oct., 1971, p. 31.
1342. *Pentecostal Evangel*, Dec. 29, 1974, p. 9.
1347. *Herald of Holiness*, Oct. 16, 1968, p. 11.
1349. *Pentecostal Evangel*, Feb. 11, 1974, p. 27.
1350. *The Link*, Dec., 1972, p. 63.
1353. *The Pulpit*, Feb., 1969, p. 25.
1354. *Moody Monthly*, Feb., 1975, p. 3.
1357. *Vital Christianity*, Sept. 8, 1974, p. 13.
1358. *Commentary*, June, 1974, p. 62.
1359. *American Opinion*, Mar., 1973, p. 95.
1360. *American Opinion*, Mar., 1973, p. 95.
1363. *Herald of Holiness*, Jan. 29, 1975, p. 5.
1364. *War Cry*, Mar. 7, 1970, p. 23.
1365. *War Cry*, Apr. 18, 1970, p. 24.
1366. *Lutheran Witness*, Nov. 3, 1974, p. 6.
1368. *Presbyterian Journal*, Jan. 22, 1975, p. 10.
1370. *Vital Christianity*, Apr. 15, 1973, p. 1.
1371. *Vital Christianity*, Oct. 15, 1972, p. 12.
1373. *Presbyterian Journal*, Aug. 14, 1974, p. 10.
1378. *Christian Herald*, Dec., 1970, p. 34.
1380. *Wesleyan Advocate*, Apr. 3, 1972, p. 6.
1381. *America*, Feb. 26, 1972.
1382. *America*, Aug. 19, 1967.
1383. *The Link*, July, 1973, p. 63.
1385. *Psychology Today*, Nov., 1972, p. 123.
1387. *The Banner*, Oct. 22, 1971, p. 15.
1390. *Presbyterian Journal*, Jan. 22, 1975, p. 7.
1391. *The Link*, Apr., 1972, p. 43.
1392. *The Banner*, Feb. 21, 1975, p. 5.
1394. *Herald of Holiness*, Nov. 7, 1973, p. 18.
1395. *American Opinion*, Nov., 1970, p. 16.
1396. *Pentecostal Evangel*, Nov. 24, 1974, p. 18.
1397. *The Link*, May, 1971, p. 34.
1400. *The Banner*, Nov. 22, 1974, p. 12.
1401. *Christianity Today*, Mar. 12, 1971, p. 6.
1402. *Herald of Holiness*, Apr. 11, 1973, p. 16.
1403. *Presbyterian Journal*, Apr. 26, 1972, p. 10.
1405. *American Opinion*, Dec., 1970, p. 72.
1406. *Herald of Holiness*, Jan. 3, 1973, p. 19.
1407. *American Opinion*, July, 1971, p. 104.
1408. *International Journal of Religious Education*, Winter, 1972, p. 9.
1409. *Watchman Examiner*, Oct. 30, 1969, p. 685.
1410. *Christianity and Crisis*, June 14, 1971, p. 118.
1411. *Lighted Pathway*, Aug., 1970, p. 25.
1412. *Church Herald*, Dec. 31, 1971, p. 10.
1414. *Eternity*, June, 1970, p. 50.

1415. *Herald of Holiness*, July 1, 1970, p. 11.
1417. *The Link*, Nov., 1972, p. 49.
1418. *Encounter*, Autumn, 1974, p. 365.
1419. *Pentecostal Evangel*, June 7, 1970, p. 10.
1420. *Pentecostal Evangel*, Oct. 20, 1974, p. 4.
1421. *Christian Life*, Oct., 1974, p. 52.
1422. *Wesleyan Advocate*, Oct. 14, 1974, p. 9.
1427. *Presbyterian Journal*, May 23, 1973, p. 7.
1428. *Christian Reader*, Apr.-May, 1973, p. 43.
1429. *His*, Jan., 1973, p. 40.
1430. *Wesleyan Advocate*, Apr. 15, 1974, p. 5.
1435. *Lutheran Witness*, Apr. 22, 1973, p. 5.
1436. *Herald of Holiness*, Oct. 11, 1972, p. 3.
1437. *Herald of Holiness*, Apr. 1, 1970, p. 6.
1439. *American Opinion*, Nov., 1971, p. 48.
1442. *The Congregationalist*, Feb., 1974, p. 6.
1444. *Herald of Holiness*, July 3, 1974, p. 12.
1445. *The Link*, May, 1974, p. 63.
1447. *His*, Jan., 1973, p. 40.
1449. *Christian Home*, July, 1974, p. 13.
1450. *Christian Herald*, Nov., 1974, p. 52.
1451. *Cross Currents*, Summer-Fall, 1972, p. 231.
1453. *Presbyterian Journal*, Mar. 24, 1971, p. 11.
1454. *Presbyterian Journal*, July 14, 1971, p. 10.
1456. *Christianity Today*, Oct. 11, 1974, p. 6.
1461. *Presbyterian Journal*, May 8, 1974, p. 13.
1462. *American Opinion*, Mar., 1974, p. 77.
1463. *The Banner*, Sept. 20, 1974, p. 14.
1466. *Wesleyan Advocate*, Feb. 7, 1972, p. 2.
1468. *Applied Christianity*, July, 1974, p. 11.
1469. *His*, June, 1974, p. 4.
1470. *American Opinion*, Dec., 1973, p. 75.
1472. *The Christian*, Oct. 20, 1968, p. 4.
1474. *American Opinion*, Sept., 1971.
1477. *Daedalus*, Fall, 1974, p. 84.
1479. *Pentecostal Evangel*, Aug. 4, 1974, p. 7.
1481. *Pentecostal Evangel*, June 1, 1973, p. 15.
1483. *Christian Century*, Mar. 1, 1967, p. 260.
1484. *Wesleyan Advocate*, Mar. 6, 1972, p. 3.
1487. *Church Herald*, Jan. 22, 1971, p. 7.
1489. *Presbyterian Journal*, Feb. 28, 1973, p. 11.
1492. *The Congregationalist*, Dec., 1970, p. 5.
1493. *The Link*, Apr., 1974, p. 63.
1494. *Watchman Examiner*, Aug. 21, 1969, p. 521.
1495. *Pentecostal Evangel*, Feb. 28, 1971, p. 4.
1496. *The Link*, Mar., 1971, p. 37.
1498. *Jewish Frontier*, Apr., 1970, p. 14.
1502. *America*, Sept. 26, 1970, p. 194.
1506. *The Banner*, Dec. 15, 1972, p. 8.
1507. *American Opinion*, Apr., 1974, p. 77.
1510. *Presbyterian Journal*, Dec. 29, 1971, p. 7.
1511. *Zygon*, June, 1974, p. 139.
1512. *The Link*, July, 1971, p. 49.
1517. *The Mennonite*, Mar. 7, 1972, p. 160.
1518. *Presbyterian Journal*, Nov. 8, 1972, p. 11.
1519. *Change*, Oct., 1974, p. 28.
1521. *Christian Century*, Oct. 10, 1973, p. 1000.
1522. *Wesleyan Advocate*, Sept. 30, 1974, p. 7.
1523. *Alliance Witness*, Jan. 22, 1969, p. 5.
1524. *Pentecostal Evangel*, Aug. 15, 1971, p. 16.
1532. *Alliance Witness*, Feb. 4, 1970, p. 10.
1533. *The Banner*, Dec. 14, 1973, p. 16.
1534. *The Link*, Jan., 1971, p. 51.
1535. *Presbyterian Journal*, June 6, 1973, p. 22.
1537. *The Banner*, Dec. 4, 1970, p. 2.
1539. *International Journal of Religious Education*, Fall, 1974, p. 20.
1540. *Pentecostal Evangel*, Mar. 24, 1974, p. 7.
1543. *Church Herald*, Oct. 4, 1974, p. 8.
1544. *American Opinion*, Apr., 1973, p. 75.
1545. *Christian Herald*, May, 1969, p. 19.
1547. *Lutheran Standard*, Oct. 28, 1969, p. 5.
1554. *American Opinion*, Dec., 1970, p. 72.
1556. *The Link*, Dec., 1970, p. 5.
1557. *The Link*, Dec., 1970, p. 58.
1558. *The Link*, Dec., 1970, p. 28.
1559. *Lutheran Standard*, Dec., 1970, p. 12.
1560. *Lutheran Witness*, Nov., 1970, p. 14.
1565. *American Opinion*, Sept., 1970, p. 89.
1566. *The Link*, Dec., 1970, p. 66.
1567. *American Opinion*, Nov., 1970, p. 70.
1568. *Christian Century*, Jan. 27, 1971, p. 99.
1572. *The Link*, Jan., 1972, p. 55.
1575. *Pentecostal Evangel*, Aug. 2, 1970, p. 4.
1576. *Vital Christianity*, May 17, 1970, p. 15.
1583. *Christianity Today*, June 4, 1971, p. 4.
1584. *His*, May, 1971, p. 5.
1586. *American Opinion*, Nov., 1971, p. 48.
1589. *American Opinion*, June, 1971, p. 71.
1590. *Lutheran Standard*, June, 1971, p. 33.
1591. *Baptist Bulletin*, Mar., 1972, p. 18.
1592. *Baptist Bulletin*, Mar., 1972, p. 18.
1593. *Christian Advocate*, Feb. 17, 1972, p. 11.
1594. *American Opinion*, Mar., 1972, p. 71.
1595. *The Link*, Mar., 1972, p. 63.
1596. *The Link*, Mar., 1972, p. 63.
1597. *The Link*, Apr., 1972, p. 43.
1602. *Presbyterian Journal*, June 28, 1972, p. 13.
1605. *The Link*, July, 1972, p. 55.
1609. *The Link*, Apr., 1973, p. 62.
1612. *Lutheran Standard*, June, 1971, p. 33.
1617. *Moody Monthly*, July-Aug., 1974, p. 63.
1621. *The Link*, Sept., 1971, p. 66.
1623. *Christian Herald*, Aug., 1972, p. 28.
1624. *American Opinion*, Mar., 1974, p. 77.
1626. *American Opinion*, Mar., 1974, p. 96.
1631. *Theology Today*, Oct., 1974, p. 184.
1633. *The Congregationalist*, June, 1973, p. 18.
1634. *The Link*, Sept., 1974, p. 59.
1635. *Theology Today*, Oct., 1974, p. 183.